with
love,
angie

1st edition
with typo's and
mistakes.

April
2022.

Published in the UK in 2022 by Joyfultraveller

Copyright © Angie Reid 2022

Angie Reid has asserted *her* right under
the Copyright, Designs and Patents Act, 1988,
to be identified as the author of this work.

Paperback ISBN 978-1-7396944-0-1
eBook ISBN 978-1-7396944-1-8

Cover design by Alan Midgley
Illustrations by Andrew Lennard
Typeset by SpiffingCovers.com

With love, angie

BY ANGIE REID

Dedication.

To Guy and Nessie my shining stars, who inspire me constantly. And now there is our beloved Karolina and Robbie.

To Kenneth, my treasured travelling companion who also, for over forty-four years, ~~Who~~ has been the kindest, most intelligent, intrepid, resourceful, forgiving and the greatest fun a Scotsman could be.

Hello Dear Readers,

This book is a collection of emails penned in different parts of the world, which I sent to my family and friends over a 16-year ~~a~~ period. Many of them have urged me to put them into ~~one~~ book, some friends have even threatened to do it for me. So, here I am, self-publishing. ~~delete~~

Coronavirus reared its ugly head in 2020 along with a hip replacement. I had time on my hands, so encouraged by my persistent family and friends, this is the result.

In 2005 we sold our family home. The beloved children had fled the nest, the house was too big and too expensive to maintain. So, we grabbed the dosh and started travelling.

That first year was spent in Spain. I was so worried that everyone would forget about me and if I'm being completely honest, it's all to do with my rather fragile ego.

I started to write these daft emails so I wouldn't be forgotten.

The Scotsman, my husband, who is the complete opposite to me, has edited my often-appalling spelling and dodgy grammar.

I am acutely aware that this is no great work of literature. I once had a little temper tantrum in front of my writing tutor, the amazing Alison Powell, "I'll never be able to write like Virginia Woolf," I said.

Quick as a flash she replied,

"Have you ever thought that Virginia Wolf wouldn't have been able to write like Angie Reid".

With love,

Angie

to: family and friends

from: Joyful Traveller

subject: Valencia, Spain. Spring 2005. A shaky start.

Dear Ones,

I got off to a rather shaky start. I managed to cry myself off to sleep last night, missing Guy and Nessie terribly. Kenneth patted my head as though I was some sort of neurotic dog, muttered something about it being all alright in the morning and, of course, it was.

I was up very early and cleaned the grimy kitchen and bathrooms. Plates covered in crusty food spilling out of the sink, a rubbish bin straining at the seams and a couple of rather large vicious looking cockroaches surveying the scene, sensing there might be trouble ahead.

Living in a student apartment may turn out to be a bit of a challenge. I left a note suggesting we might have a cleaning rota. Who am I kidding? I was at least thirty years old before I'd finally worked out what a squeezy mop was for. As I was doing my bit of scrubbing, it did go through my mind at one point that they might really loathe this middle-aged, rubber gloved wielding English woman - but the opposite has happened.

Marcia, a 19-year-old French girl, practically fell into my arms. She is missing her parents hugely and now so pleased someone like her mother will be living with her. So much for the laid-back, student attitude I'm trying to adopt!

Sven, a Danish computer programmer, terribly proper and serious of nature appeared in the doorway. He's long and thin and I have a feeling he's a bit adverse to smiling but extremely taken with my efforts and insists on being responsible for the cleaning rota. We even discussed what meals we might cook together.

Lulu hasn't appeared yet; I fancy she's a bit of a wild one.

Later, Marcia manoeuvred me into a corner and unburdened herself, spilling out her woeful love life.

This morning at the language school we had an introductory session. There were lots of clever looking types, eager and full of energy. I sat there feeling a bit ancient and realised I'd left my pen at home.

At lunch time I had a large glass of wine with my salami roll. I was hoping it might give me some Dutch courage - pity it wasn't Spanish.

More to come,

With love,

Angie

to: family and friends

from: Joyful Traveller

subject: Valencia - Three weeks later and hanging on in there.

Dearest Ones,

I'm still here, red-faced and hanging on by the skin of my teeth. I can beautifully recite many Spanish verbs but putting them into practice is altogether another matter. Meanwhile the Scotsman appears to be making huge progress. He's the type who seems to be able to do anything, when he sets his mind to it. It's an attractive quality, only wish some of it would rub off on me.

I have managed to do three whole weeks without shedding a single tear. My classmates are a particularly attractive lot. The sweetest girl, Catherine Grenville-Jones, sits on my right; an army officer's daughter who constantly gees me up with platitudes such as:

"We can do this Angie, we can get through this together". She happens to have just left Nottingham University where she got a 1st in chemical engineering - a tender 23-year-old with a photographic memory.

On my left is Francisco. A handsome, charming Portuguese lad who loves his Mamma dearly. He watches every move of my pen then jabs me in the ribs when I get it wrong, which happens all the time. He lets me see his work and urges me to copy it.

"Francisco this is cheating",

"Everyone cheats, Angie, what's the big deal?"

Unfortunately, I'm not bright enough to figure out what is Portuguese and what is Spanish, so now I seem to be learning two languages.

A tiny little Japanese girl is next along, so small and fragile. She comes and stands very close to me during our coffee breaks.

I think she sees me as this great Amazonian who will protect her. She has no English. Our exchanges consist of heaps of face pulling and odd arm movements. I long to put my arms around her but I know this is not the correct thing to do, I'm careful not to offend her. I think she might spend her entire time praying that Francisco will keep himself to himself, although he rarely does.

Valencia is rather gorgeous. The Old Quarter feels ancient and full of souls who have gone before. It's all so .....well, so Spanish, with very little English spoken and traditions that have weaved through the centuries are still active and important today. There are constant festivals and processions throughout the city. A chosen clutch of city elders wonderfully named, The Council of the Wise Men of the Plain of Murcia still meet each Thursday in the cathedral vestry to 'orally settle disputes about water rationing in a swift, transparent and impartial manner'.

Warm honey-coloured buildings, tall and imposing crowd together down a maze of winding cobbled alleyways and back streets. All at once, the sun is there as you enter pretty squares laden with the smell of japonica and magnolia which vie with the scent of orange blossom. A church, large or small, appears on almost every corner.

Giant colourful murals collide with smaller pieces of street art. There's an edge to this city; maybe it's the graffiti which is abundant, comical, political, fierce at times - perhaps that's what gives this city an undercurrent of excitement and just a whiff of danger.

The old, dried-up riverbed which runs through the centre of the city has been cleverly and thoughtfully converted into a glorious green recreational ribbon containing sports pitches, picnic areas, benches, running tracks and bike lanes. Tourists clamber aboard four-seater quadracycles. I love watching these contraptions on which everyone is supposed to pedal. Some sneaky types who appear to be working hard pushing their pedals are doing nothing of the sort. They're just freeloading. I did that, the Scotsman wasn't impressed.

Kenneth and I are trying to get fit. We huff and puff our way up to the riverbed each day, him in his Asda trainers, me with my bosoms bobbing up and down. What a sight. I've got all the gear on. Heart rate monitor, pedometer, running shoes, jogging bottoms, portable radio - you name it, I've got it. It doesn't seem to make a scrap of difference. Kenneth still has that cuddly tummy and my bottom still jiggles. Maybe it's those coffees and pastries we stop off for every morning.

I was awake all last night thinking of the children.

Guy, deeply immersed in his books, the university he chose seems to fit him like a glove. S.O.A.S.-The School of Oriental and African Studies. Where else could he study Buddhism. His mind is like a sponge, soaking up knowledge which he's done from a tiny tot. As I lay there, I had a little giggle wondering how the teaching staff were coping with him. He managed to get nodules on his vocal cords, very, very few six-year-old develop them. Opera singers and folk who use their voices a great deal tend to suffer. Well, this six-year-old developed nodules. He was so excited and so desperate to know everything the world had to offer; he would forget to breath before talking. We ended up having to have 'quiet times' throughout the day, bet that's not happening now.

Nessie sent photos. She's now in deepest Northern India. She's on a camel in the desert, sleeping under the stars, brown as a berry and dressed from head to foot in swirling silk. A wild, adventurous soul. She's loving every exciting, scary, life-enhancing adventure. I think of the phrase I read not long ago, "Life is a balance between holding on and letting go" and I'm trying very hard to let go.

With love,

Angie

* (part of the University of London)

There is something very strange about the water in Valencia. I started off looking quite chic; my hair now resembles a disorganised straw bale coupled with a face that has taken on the look of someone a bit demented.

I've adopted this look so I can get through my days at the language school praying the teachers don't ask me to read aloud, heaven help me, or enquire about my knowledge of Spanish verbs.

Everyone, and I mean everyone, seems to understand what is going on in the classroom. I sit there totally bewildered. I've figured out the best way to deal with this is just to grin. So, I grin and grin and now I can't stop. This attitude is definitely making me feel a little better but having very little influence on my language learning.

I hate it all and couldn't care less about the subjunctive, the placement of prepositions and the past, present and future tenses. I'd much rather be sitting outside in the sunshine happily watching the world go by.

Never ask your partner/husband to teach you, especially sodding Spanish verbs. Poor Kenneth, usually such a happy chap.............

A bit of a challenge this, more later.

With love,

Angie

to: family and friends

from: Joyful Traveller

subject: Valencia - Must try harder.

Dear Ones,

Haven't had time to write my missives as have had so much homework, most of which I haven't managed to do.

It's been a roller coaster of emotions. From the start, as I entered the door of the language school, I knew it was going to be a bit of a disaster. Meeting the other students, fresh faced and confident only added to my fears.

This week there appears to be a huge influx of Swedes. As they arrive, my newly found young friends move up to another class leaving me behind.

The Swedish students command of the English language is so good, probably better than mine.

They are long limbed, tousled blondes with the whitest teeth and stunningly gorgeous. By the time I had arranged my pen and pad and various bit of paper from the previous classes, I seemed to have missed half the session.

Collectively, they needed to hear a new word or phrase only once and that was that: they remembered it. I meanwhile was still farting around with my paper and then my dyslexia kicked in. Breathe. I did lots of deep breathing. I'm sure they must have thought I was having 'a turn' as my face grew redder and redder with every minute while ineffectually practising my yogic breathing.

I was transported back to my unhappy school days. Remember streaming in schools? The underachievers either never moved up a grade or were placed in the D section or sometimes put back a year. Not long ago while going through my Mother's papers I unearthed some of my old school reports. I wondered why she had kept them; they all said the same gloomy things:

"Angela permanently appears to have her head firmly in the clouds"

"Angela's attention span seems very short and seems to be growing shorter by the term".

…….and the good old tried and tested one,

"Angela must try harder".

I sat in the classroom surrounded by all these young things and I felt so despondent. All that horribleness of school, all those hateful lessons. Long remembered feelings of inadequacy came tumbling out and the more I tried the worse it became.

The English, on the whole, are hopeless when it comes to languages. I know that's a huge generalisation but I'm wondering now if it's something genetic.

After many tears and tantrums and a very bruised ego I have left the classes and for a few weeks I now have individual lessons with the Head of School, no less. I don't think they've encountered anyone quite so melodramatic and hopeless as me.

The Scotsman, of course, is going from strength to strength.

Besos (kisses) and muchos abrazos (many hugs) almost stretches my Spanish to the limit.

I'm not going to sign off just yet though, so on a happier note, let me tell you about the food which is now firmly making a play for my middle. I defy anyone here to be on a miserable calorie-controlled diet.

Sundays are still special days in Spain usually shared with family or close friends. Here in Valencia, as if by magic, the busy bustling streets become deserted just before the stroke of 2pm then hordes of people cram into restaurants. Multi generations, best frocks, Sunday suits, little boys in sailor outfits and girls in frilly dresses. Paella is the Sunday lunch. Huge pans of it adorn each table followed by a free for all as each member of the family tucks in. A truly sharing dish.

It all started over 1,500 years ago when the invading Moors introduced rice to Valencia. Hungry farmers often with only one big shallow pan to their name would prepare their lunch in the fields by chucking anything they could find into the pan. Rice, broad beans and rabbit were staples along with snails that clung to the wild rosemary and thyme bushes. Meat, seafood and assorted vegetables were introduced later. The shallow, open pans were perfect for quick cooking while enabling any water to evaporate. The best bits were, and still are the caramelized, crispy grains that stick to the bottom of the pan. Valencianos only eat paella for lunch or during the day; never in the evening – that's left to the tourists.

The rest of the week is taken up with other gastronomic delights. We head off to the Mercado Central, one of the largest and most impressive covered markets in Europe, and each time the conversation goes something like this:

"This time we must only buy what's written on the list". Kenneth's list, of course, - he's a list sort of man. I make lists, write them out meticulously then leave them on the kitchen table or put them into the wrong pocket.

"Yes, only what's on the list". Last time it was almost impossible to carry everything back to the flat. (The Scotsman still has this unnerving aversion to taxis).

We get to the market, eyes glazing over as they start roaming around the counters wanting to buy every delicious, gorgeous piece of scrumptiousness we spy. Bags of gleaming salted roasted almonds, plump terracotta-coloured figs, vast fiery red tomatoes, slabs of buttery Manchego cheese, great sides of Iberian ham hanging like Christmas decorations, outlandish fish and seafood of every shape and size. We watched as a very old lady wrestled a live lobster into her canvas bag. They tie the claws up with rubber bands but this lobster was not going down without a fight. Her bag was dancing from side to side as she left the market. I wondered if she was getting on a bus. Imagine having to sit next to a carrier bag snapping and squirming all around the place.

We leave the market with bags heaving, shopping list long forgotten. We need sustenance before the heavy trek home. We sit at the bar vowing not to order too much food, we always do. Plates of roasted piquillo peppers stuffed full of bechamel and tuna drip off the plate, marinated anchovies salty and tasty, small olives black and inviting, big fat green ones covered in fragrant olive oil and the ubiquitous patatas bravas - chunks of perfectly roasted potatoes laced with a rich tomato sauce crowned with garlic aioli and a slash of searing orange paprika, that can sometimes take the roof of your mouth off. On the side, there are chunks of crisp white bread and a salad which, strangely, always seems to contain tinned tuna, asparagus spears and sweet corn nestling among leaves of bright green lettuce.

For pudding, it's always flan, a kind of crème caramel, topped off with a carajillo. This is a strong dark café espresso, laced with Spanish brandy.

Sometimes if we are feeling a little more energetic, we might make it to the sardine cupboard. A small, narrow space hosting a bar and a few stools and the tiniest of loos you could ever imagine. There's no space to bend even a little so you have to almost stand up to pee. We go there so often, I've become quite adapt at this.

Two enterprising brothers run this busy operation. One briskly takes the orders and pours the wine, the other cooks on a tiny gas ring the size of two dinner plates producing the most delicious sardines you could ever imagine. Dripping in olive oil, covered in lightly roasted garlic, fat, juicy sardines fly off the plates. Rough, red local wine is served in small glasses alongside tiny dishes of salted almonds.

Hot chocolate and churros are a treat, - becoming too much of a treat I notice. I can't describe them now to you as I'm starving and just thinking of them my mouth is watering, just to say churros are a big, fat, delicious sort of doughnut....a bit like me at the moment.

With love,

Angie

Hello Everyone,

Yippee....my Spanish course comes to an end on Friday.

Have now been taught by every single teacher in the school. Don't think anyone has ever achieved this. Usually, you have two teachers and stick with them throughout your time there. They have all been wonderful, long suffering and terribly kind. I've turned into a little institution all on my own. I've even been given a few lessons by the principle himself. A lovely kind man whose patience I think I have destroyed. *Principal*

His name is Carlos, he's very thin and wiry and concerned.

"Angie" he says, with his brow creased like rumpled tissue paper.

"Angie" another deep sigh emits from the depths of his being. I kid you not, it's all rather dramatic and I'm trying not to smile but squirming under the table.

"Do you ever do your homework?" He knows the answer of course and leaves me little room to make up some pitiful lie. Of course I don't do the homework. We live with all these gorgeous young creatures who, surprisingly, seem to want my company. It's a hard decision; stay in and do the boring homework or drink delicious mojitos while learning how to salsa.

To save this dear man anymore embarrassment I suggest I have a little break and review the situation. Carlos now starts to smile, something that has been missing from our many exchanges.

"Angie, you are very welcome to return at any time. Learning a language requires much effort".

I continue to smile as an unsaid message flutters by.

"We will be very sorry to see you leave".

He hugs me tight and kisses me warmly on both my cheeks but as he arises, I notice a little jaunty step and a brow that is no longer so creased.

I might have found a wonderful new way to learn the language. Met a charming Spanish girl who speaks perfect English. She took me to see this mad artist. Walked into his studio and instantly fell in love with the place. Paint everywhere, opera playing so loud it could burst your ear drums. It sits right in the heart of Barrio Carmen - the ancient, gothic, arty, bohemian area. A higgledy-piggledy place with medieval-looking buildings that look as though they are about to topple down.

A man 'with attitude' would be an apt description. He was scathing and thoroughly unpleasant but I wanted so badly to learn how to draw by then, anything other than returning to the dreaded language school.

He eyed me up and told my friend he'd only "take me on" if I had any talent. I've only got a modicum of talent so I knew I would have to find another route. Decided my enthusiasm was the only plus factor in all of this.

I could understand him if I concentrated very hard. He spoke not one word of English.

It's amazing what you can do when you really want to. I worked so hard that first session and, unbelievably, when he barked his orders out, I must have followed them. At the end of that class he muttered something like, "Si".

I've been back six times so far. He makes me do the most complicated and difficult exercises. At the end of my last class he grudgingly said out of one corner of his mouth, "Bueno" scowled a bit more then dismissed me with an unpleasant wave of his hand - but I did notice a slight upturn at the corners of his mouth.

I arrive back at the apartment covered in charcoal, blissfully happy.

It can be a little unnerving this student life, never quite sure who you will be living with. Remember the two cockroaches I'd spied happily capering around the edges of the table when we first arrived? Dirty dishes piled high, waste bins spilling their dirt.

I was a complete and utter slob as a student only washing a dish when every piece of crockery had been used. Leaving rubbish bins so chock full that when I tried to release the plastic bags from their containers, they would split open leaving a trail of dirty, smelly stuff behind them and what was so astonishing, I kept doing it.

We couldn't live in this filth so I came up with a plan. I have a friend, a graphic artist. He produced a set of drawings depicting cockroaches in the worst possible light, foul and ugly, some had even made their way under sheets and pillowcases. I positioned these nauseating sketches in strategic points around the flat. Not a dirty dish, smelly sock or grime-filled bin in sight nowadays!

Our student flat has changed. Shelly from Manchester left on Saturday. "You've been just like an older sister to me" said through many tears. Quite a compliment as I'm older than her mother. In her place is a suave Austrian doctor. Extremely handsome and flirts outrageously. He has that air of entitlement, probably been spoilt all his life but something saves him from being a real prat. He has a considerable interest in people. He's probably an extremely caring and compassionate doctor. Shame he's only staying for a week.

We still have Marcia from France who often sits on my bed and cries; she has a bit of a disastrous love life. Stev our cool Dane, is beginning to open up. I get the impression he loves the order that has been created in the flat and he can often be seen cheerfully wielding a dustpan and brush. Lulu from Belgium, frightfully studious in the daytime but by nightfall she's dancing on the table surrounded by empty bottles of wine. We all rub along nicely.

The Scotsman, surrounded by horrid language manuals and numerous notebooks, is happily looking forward to the start of his ADVANCED Spanish course. He's such a geek, but a very happy one as he waves me off on my evening adventures.

With love,

Angie

to: family and friends

from: Joyful Traveller

subject: Valencia - Las Fallas and a partying 90-year-old

Las Fallas takes place in March every year, nineteen days of utter madness. No one is quite sure when it started, some say back in The Middle Ages. A festival celebrating Saint Joseph, the patron saint of carpenters and the arrival of Spring. Out with the old and in with the new. Carpenters, working in short winter days, needed light to work by when daylight disappeared. They would have planks of wood attached to which would be candles and oil lamps giving them enough light to be able to carry on working.

Spring arrived and these pieces of wood were discarded and burnt. Children started to beg neighbours for bits of fabric, old rugs, anything that could be used as a decoration. Soon figures were fashioned, becoming more elaborate as time went by.

Today they are gigantic works of art, some taller than buildings and many having to be winched into place by massive cranes. The figures are acutely political, often salacious and wickedly entertaining. Local celebrities and politicians are often up for ridicule.

Over seven hundred and fifty Fallas and ninots (exhibits and puppets) were built this year. At midnight on the 19th March they all went up in flames – all except one; the best is saved and that proudly goes into the Fallas museum.

We heard this story, I don't know how true it is, but it makes a good tale. Firefighters from all over Europe are invited to help when the burning takes place. Crowds gather and not until the very last part of the edifice is burnt to the ground do they leave, happy in the knowledge that the ritual has been completed - crucial for the happiness and health of the upcoming year. It was a German firefighting team who were on duty at one of the events this night. Being extra organized and highly vigilant they leapt into action with their mammoth hose pipes and proceeded to extinguish the burning effigy long before it was fully burnt. The crowd was horror-struck, beside themselves with rage, almost causing a riot.

The German firefighters have never been invited back.

Each area of the city has its own Fallas association, usually with its own brass band, and as soon as one Fallas season is over they start planning for the next one. Walking through the streets you suddenly come across vast tables, decorated and laid for numerous people. Large cavernous rooms and street marquees teem with people of all ages drinking and eating and always an enormous paella cooking on a huge burner in the middle of the street. Men stand around looking frightfully important wearing neckerchiefs that denote the area they belong to. Catching up with the latest news; people watching locals and visitors alike; gesticulating with extravagant body language; stirring great vats of rice - and if they like the look of you, you might get lucky and be offered a glass of wine and a tale of Fallas history.

The Flower offering to The Virgin takes place over the last two days. Thousands of mostly women, often with children and babies in pushchairs parade through the streets. The women carry vividly coloured bouquets of flowers.

It's curiously emotional watching the endless procession. There is a quiet seriousness and a dignity that surrounds it. Mile upon mile of brightly coloured, highly decorated Falleras, the local women in traditional dress, walk with heads held high to the Plaza de la Virgen. There, a 14-metre wooden structure representing the Virgin is decorated with the flower offerings carried by the women. The air is heady and heavy with the smell of a sea of flowers. It is all so very beautiful.

The Mascletà, the wackiest thing you could ever imagine, takes place dead on 2pm every day from the 1st to the 19th of March. Hundreds of kilos of gunpowder explode in the middle of the Town Hall Square. The sound is so deafening your ear drums feel as though they are about to explode. Locals proudly stand and appear to revere the whole crazy spectacle. Apparently, if you open your mouth slightly, it's supposed to help avoid the deafness that might follow but if you are left deaf for a few minutes after this spectacle then the pyrotechnics have done their job well. My hearing didn't come back until we'd staggered two roads back and then everything felt as though there was a fog around me.

The burnings began at midnight. Huge effigies were burnt alongside magnificent fireworks displays and booming music. The city had exploded. We crawled back home towards sunrise, smelling of smoke and sticky with doughnuts and hot chocolate laced with brandy. Passing a group of elegantly dressed ladies, probably in their seventies, Kenneth overheard one lady turn to another and say, "I'm a bit worried about my mother; I wonder where she is and what she's up to?".

I had visions of a ninety-year-old partying in the street, refusing to go home and behave herself. Just hope I might be like that one day.

With love,

Angie

to: family and friends

from: Joyful Traveller

subject: Valencia - Two wonderful gentlemen

Hello Everyone,

My hair has not gone according to plan. Unfortunately, it started to turn a rather strange shade of pink. Fine on a lovely young thing but I look decidedly peculiar as though I've had trouble with some electrical appliance that has singed my hair - or I'm trying the Punk look.

This time a different hairdresser. I should have seen the warning signs. This is exactly what he looked like, I promise you. He sported extremely tight trousers, a shirt unbuttoned revealing lots of chest hair complete with handfuls of gold jewellery. The jewellery was in competition with his long, luxuriant hair. Both would sway back and forth as he wielded his scissors.

I still don't speak any Spanish and he no English, so I emerged from his salon with what can only be described as a rather nasty-looking cowpat on my head. Convinced people were looking at me, I went out and bought a very large, very dark pair of sunglasses. I've taken to wearing them all the time and have had several spells of tripping over at night, as my vision has become rather impaired now.

The Spanish do some things wonderfully well: eat, drink, talk and smoke and then do it all over again - but hairdressers, they do not.

Meanwhile, Arif and Alexandre have created a marvellous restaurant. We met them just by chance through one of the students at the language school and I know they are going to be our best friends for life. Everything is perfect, from the elegant tables, all in different shades of grey, so chic and easy on the eye to the lusciously delicious food.

Arif, in a kitchen the size of a small cupboard. He was born in

England, the son of Pakistani parents, and his food is influenced by both cultures. Add Middle Eastern and Spanish flavours and it's almost like the world on your plate, each dish is a gastronomic joy. I look at the menu in an agitated state the problem being that I want to order well, ... everything. Knowing how much planning and preparation has gone into each plate of food just adds to my dilemma. Next time, I might just close my eyes and stab the menu blindfolded.

Alexandre is French and watching him is like watching a scene from a ballet. He glides elegantly from table to table, charming and chatting to everyone he comes into contact with (he speaks at least four languages fluently). He's interested in everyone and everything and his passion for the menu is infectious.

Once in a while, there is something almost self-indulgently decadent about sitting alone and eating delicious food. I do this while Kenneth is away with Guy. There's no conversation, no distractions, just the mindful joy of savouring every mouthful. It's so easy to just shovel food into your mouth without thinking or truly savouring it and, often in my case, talking all the time.

They are the most affectionate of friends. Warm and charming and huge fun. Going for coffee with them tomorrow, wish they'd invite me to live with them.

Went clothes shopping today, very depressing. Spanish shops seem to cater for flat-chested women. Everything is either too tight or hangs down in a way that makes me look like a large beach ball.

I have become friendly with the lady who runs the Internet café. She is trying to improve her English. We started out very happily with a mixture Spanish and English but she seems to have given up on my Spanish. She sinks into a bit of a concerned and then depressive mood when I try speaking her mother tongue and now, especially with the cowpat, she tends not to look at me much.

With love,

Angie

to: family and friends

from: Joyful Traveller

subject: Valencia - The good and the bad.

Hi Everyone,

We left Valencia on a sunny Sunday morning for a little jaunt into the countryside to be followed by a night stop at a rustic B&B. It was one of those mornings when the sun can't seem to stop itself from invading every spare inch of space. We'd eaten a delicious breakfast. One you long to reproduce at home but can never quite manage it. What could be simpler than roasted red tomatoes on toast? Those tomatoes with their mouth-bursting richness sat on a crispy sourdough concoction. Rustic and chic at the same time – irresistible.

We drove down a wide avenue lined with ancient trees sprawling over the road forming a canopy, creating welcome shade as the sun rose higher in the sky. We heard a toot and there alongside our car were two young men in theirs. Handsome faces with lots of curly dark hair and such concerned looks. They kept pointing to the front tyre with an anxious look on their faces. Thanking them with smiles and gestures we turned into a small side street and stopped to investigate.

I remember wittering on to Kenneth after this encounter, "People are so kind, how nice was that".

Then an equally nice character who just happened to be passing on his bicycle stopped and he, too, seemed to be very concerned. He started chatting to Kenneth and called to me, indicating I should get out of my seat and have a look.

He examined the tyre with much care and thought, told us he believed it had been slashed on purpose. He indicated a garage which was not far away and then he was on his merry way.

Again, I waffled on, "Well, how kind was that and who would slash our tyre? What a nice young chap".

You can tell where this is all leading, can't you?

I got back into the car. Whenever I get a bit flustered or when things aren't going too well, I tend to reach for my lipstick. There's something rather soothing about applying lipstick, it must be the action of plastering it backwards and forwards over your lips.

"Where's my handbag Kenneth? Did you move it?"

My handbag contained lipsticks, credit cards, diary and various vitally important objects like tweezers and allergy tablets and sunscreen lotion and my best, my very bestest favourite pair of sunglasses which I have managed not to lose for years and years and years.

"Kenneth what did you do with it?".

Then, the penny dropped and there's a sinking feeling that engulfs you. It starts at your feet and slowly, methodically makes its way up through your body. By the time it gets to your face it is replaced by absolute rage. We'd been scammed.

"Those bloody little shits".

You go over and over in minute detail how it could have happened. How, from the beginning, they were working as a gang each one playing his nasty little part. Then you realise with a jolt of disgust there was a fourth person you didn't even clap eyes on, the one who stole my handbag while that ever so nice young man kept us talking. It does make the rose-tinted spectacles you've been wearing turn a nasty shade of vermilion

After all the poncing around (fitting the spare tyre, cancelling credit cards, calling the bank, a long-drawn-out visit to the local police station), I did have a little smirk. Okay, they got my rather nice handbag and my sunglasses and a couple of gorgeous lipsticks and, by now, worthless credit cards. Kenneth often gets a bit crabby with me as I never seem to have any cash. He often tells me, "You're just like the Queen", apparently, she never has any dosh on her, and this time, neither did I.

When we arrived at a little village late that afternoon we were both feeling despondent and a bit grubby. When people behave badly it somehow rubs off on you. If I'd thought stealing my handbag had helped a worthy cause I wouldn't have felt so miserable, but I kept seeing those two young men in their flashy, expensive car. The boy on the bike was charming and articulate and even I could understand a little of what he was saying. I wonder where the fourth one came from. He must have been lurking in the bushes nearby then pounced when he saw his opportunity.

The sun was getting low in the sky when we passed a sign, 'GARAJE', written in large bold bright red letters. Below it, was an open door and there sat a gentleman dressed in his Sunday best. He was perched on an old wooden chair in the late afternoon sun puffing on a cigarette.

He greeted us like old friends and when Kenneth related the tale of the slashed tyre, he almost cried. Tomorrow morning, early as we liked, he would fit a new tyre. Our small guest house was only a short distance up the road; he knew it well. He insisted that we join him for a glass of wine. Producing two ancient wobbly iron chairs and two dusty glasses he proceeded to fill with wine, made from grapes that his son-in-law grew a couple of fields away. He was very sympathetic about our unfortunate experience and then he recalled a rather harrowing story similar to ours, but this time the thieves jumped into the car and drove off with it, not realising there was a baby strapped in the back seat. The baby, he assured us, was unharmed and found only a few miles away where the car had been abandoned. I couldn't stop thinking about the terror the mother must have felt when they drove off with her baby – and then the shock the thieves must have got when they turned around and saw a baby sat there.

True to his word, the next morning he supplied a new tyre and at a huge discount. When Kenneth queried him about the low price he had charged us, he simply folded his arms and smiled. I think it was a generous gesture, on his part, trying to make us feel better for what had happened.

We drove off after many hugs and kisses only to discover a rattling sound coming from the boot. When we stopped a few yards up the road, we found two huge bottles of his son-in-law's wine, it had been placed alongside our suitcases together with a big, fat, home-made chorizo.

With love,

Angie

to:	family and friends
from:	Joyful Traveller
subject:	Valencia - Sexy Spanish estate agents

Tentatively looking for an apartment. Do I really want to live here full-time? I'm not sure but looking for a property here is not quite the same as looking for one at home.

We went to view a place by the beach. Waited and waited, no one turned up. A elderly, rather fraught looking lady poked her head out of the next-door window and proceeded to shout at the top of her voice. I was listening but, of course, didn't understand a word that she said. A look of sympathy and then irritation crept over Kenneth's face. The whole row of houses was due to be demolished in a couple of weeks' times, this lady was being turfed out and we should, "Vete a al mierda" - basically, "fuck off". If she had had a bucket of water to hand to throw over us, she probably would have, quite happily.

The extremely handsome but forgetful estate agent then turned up - without the key - looking like a Vogue model, dressed from head to foot in designer black with an attractive stubbly chin. But, I fear he was in the wrong job. Assuring us that what we had heard was untrue he persuaded us to wait for him as he dashed off into the street. The thought of living next door to the harridan wasn't very appealing but Kenneth wanted to wait, so we did.

We had to go and have a cup of coffee while he returned to his office to find the key to a place that was going to be demolished. He returned a while later; the apartment was no longer available. When we suggested it could be because it was going to be destroyed soon, he looked very uncomfortable and just shrugged his handsome shoulders.

At another meeting, we encountered a charming but hugely disorganised estate agent who drove us around for an hour and a quarter. She too, was dressed in the most gorgeous black outfit, so tight around her marvellous bottom and wearing the highest of black shoes with tiny diamanté studs running up the back of her heels. If I were to wear that I'd look outrageous but somehow the Spanish and Italian women I know can get away with it. They look sexy and gorgeous. Maybe it's something to do with owning your curves, enjoying the feminine, being safe in your own body, having fun. But she had no idea where the flat was which she was supposed to be selling. We spent an age driving round and round then, gave up, and we all went for a drink. She told me how much she loved meeting new people but wasn't so keen on the house selling side of the job.

Miss you all so much. Will be ready to come home for the summer.

With love,

Angie

to: family and friends

from: Joyful Traveller

subject: Summer 2006 - Andalusia. The rain in Spain…..

Here we are house-sitting in the depths of Andalusia.

It's supposed to rain for sixty-five days of the year in this part of Spain. I think most of it has fallen on us in the last couple of weeks. Back home you have all been basking in the sunshine while we have been frozen up this mountain - a few warm days, just a few, the rest have been cold and wet.

Today, I didn't think we would make it down the hillside. The truck spun all over the place, careering into the sides of the track, spinning wheels that appeared to take on a maniacal life of their own. The mud reached the windscreen and when we put the wipers on, they magnificently smeared it everywhere until we were sat with a brown sheet of sludge covering the entire windscreen. Oddly, it had stopped raining and with no water in the vehicle The Scotsman, who was responsible for getting us moving, requested I go and find something to clean the windscreen with. Up a mountain, I don't normally bother to dress up but we were going into the small village today.

I must be turning into my glorious grandmother. It was impossible for her to leave the house without full makeup and at least one piece of jewellery. Nana was ninety-two years old with hardly a day's illness in her life. So, when my aunt called and told us she had been taken into hospital I began to panic, fearing the worst. Rushing in, there she was sat upright, regal and a bit bothered. I noticed someone had scored out her Christian name and replaced this with Mrs. This was a lady who insisted on being addressed in the correct manner all her life, even at the end of it.

"My darling one, oh dear, oh dear girl I am so very upset"

Thinking maybe the doctors had found some inoperable tumour or a condition they couldn't treat, my heart started pounding and I could feel tears welling up behind my eyes. This was a woman I adored. This was the lady I had confided in so many times knowing she would never judge, knowing she had led a wild, selfish and joyful life, knowing nothing could shock her.

"Nana, what is it?"

I took her perfectly manicured hand and held it tight. Too tight as she released it quickly and in an agitated voice said,

"Your aunt" (my long-suffering aunt who lived nearby) has brought in the wrong shade of lipstick".

The next day this fiercely beloved grandmother of mine was dead - but she had died wearing the right shade of lipstick.

Getting back to soggy Spain. There we were stuck halfway down a mountainside with no way of moving until we could see out of the window. I had on a rather nice pair of cream linen culottes, beige brogues and a light blue cashmere cardigan. As I stumbled and fell into a ditch all I could think about was how I could kill Kenneth.

As I emerged from the ditch, which had been cleverly camouflaged with lots of vegetation, I could hear laughter. Two outbreaks of laughter. One seemed to be coming from the truck and the other from across the hedge. There, across the shrubbery, was the rotund, bad-tempered farmer we had previously come across with his nasty dogs. He was chewing on a grubby stick and his ruddy red face was contorted with mirth. I mustered all my dignity, aware of the brown muck that was now trailing down my face, and I smiled as calmly and as gracefully as I could. The jolly farmer was having none of it, he called his dogs and they came for me, snapping at my feet, trying to fell me for a second time. I grimaced and squelched myself back into the truck with the laughing Scotsman rocking back and forth unable to contain himself. The heavens opened and the windscreen cleared.

The open fire in the sitting room smokes so much you end up unable to see your hand in front of your face so, instead, we sit huddled around the stove in the kitchen. Kenneth, of course, being the outdoorsy Scotsman he is, loves it all. I meanwhile, am permanently attached to my hot-water bottle.

It's been a bit of a test of character and also of a marriage. We only have ourselves and two smelly old cats for company and a couple of guinea pigs that love to bite me. Occasionally, another old farmer, without teeth, will appear with wild asparagus. We think it is a present. We're in a bit of a quandary; should we offer him any money? We don't want to offend him but neither do we want to appear mean. He tills the soil with the most ancient of tractors in a field just up the lane from us. The problem is that neither of us can understand a word he says. I think he's probably a gentle, kind man but there are deeply ingrained lines on his face; years of hardship and struggle seem to cry out. He has a battered old hat, full of little holes which are gradually morphing into one another. This makes his hat sit at a jaunty angle on his head, greatly at odds with his demeanour.

I offered him a cup of tea the other day. He looked longing at the cup but sadly shook his head and wandered off. We have decided that baking is the answer. Sadly, my culinary skills have not improved so Kenneth will do the baking. Cake is always a marvellous gift - one that doesn't require any language skills.

When the generator is running (there is no mains electricity) I hook-up my computer to the BBC and listen to The Archers.

It was the time of year again when Race for Life was taking place in Bristol. The first one - eight years ago - I did with my beloved sister, Libby. After her death, I vowed I would continue to do it every year with Lucy. Lucy my precious niece was disappointed I wouldn't be there with her this year. I decided I would have to do it on my own here, up a Spanish mountain, so she would know I was with her in spirit.

I'd worked out a route and set my pedometer. Five kilometres was doable until I came across the dogs. What is it about the Spanish who live in the countryside and their dogs? They either insist on tying them up for hours - often days - at a time or they let these furious, ferocious dogs run loose. Walking past farmhouses, barns and assorted outhouses that appeared to be derelict I would pray the gates were closed and the wild barking I could hear was coming from an animal that couldn't reach me and maul me to death. Last year, I heard about a French woman who was out walking in the mountains on her own. She lasted a month, after being savaged by Spanish dogs, before dying.

I was determined to complete this walk; no dog was going to deter me. In the end, it was a little ankle-biter that had me retreating back up the path, an ugly, pug-faced terrier-type with sharp incisors and an unpleasant manner. I legged it but soon realised I'd have to return the same way, there was no other way home. After two and a half kilometres I turned to face the beast. There he was in wait for me, spread out with his head resting on his front paws. By now, the sun was hot and he seemed a little exhausted, I realised he was an old boy. I approached him armed with my water bottle and a rather naff stick that had splintered as my journey had progressed. He watched me intently, peering out from under his bushy eyebrows. It seemed we had come to an unspoken understanding, him and me. So long as I walked by sharpish, he didn't have to do all that snapping and snarling business and trying to look important. We had the measure of each other - respect.

A bit of a different walk to my usual route around The Downs in Bristol, but I had completed it, and somewhere up there was Libby having a good laugh.

With love as always - and if you have any spare dosh, chuck it in the direction of Race for Life.

Angie

to: family and friends

from: Joyful Traveller

subject: Buenos Aires, Argentina – 2007.
          A chance encounter never to forget.

I'm on first name terms with a delightful, aging man at the Internet café located just under our apartment. He smiles broadly every time I visit. He watches me while I read my emails. He's a man who appears to be interested in everyone and everything. We had a long talk yesterday on the nature of love. I think he might love everyone.

He'll probably start kissing me soon. Everyone kisses everyone here, even the bin men when they greet each other in the mornings. Quite extraordinary to watch them give each other a great smacker on the cheek.

One of my little expeditions to the shoe shop resulted in lots of kissing after I purchased a pair of sandals. It's not your everyday-type kissing, it's really decent kissing, as though you might be kissing a close friend.

Buenos Aires is exciting, humid, noisy, dirty and full of wonderfully warm and extraordinarily friendly people. They are a generous lot even though their history is littered with anguish and pain.

The place is deranged and beautiful and intoxicating and, yes, they do dance in the streets. A sexy type of tango ending with a long lingering kiss. How good it is to watch seventy, eighty-year-olds being seductive, flirting with each other like there is no tomorrow. For many Argentinians their tomorrows were bleak and full of foreboding.

Everything came crashing down in 2001. Many of the middle classes lost their homes, their saving, their jobs. The country was in crisis. A liberal Argentinian journalist believes it stemmed from a rather haughty clique of Argentinians, who thought they were part of a European country (over seven million Europeans emigrated here between 1850 and 1950) then suddenly realising they weren't and now a grudging acceptance that they are now part of volatile Latin America.

There is a fitting description in a book I'm reading at the moment, written by an Argentinian journalist describing his countrymen. "A people who instinctively know that the line dividing tragedy and farce is a fine one".

They are still aware the economy is on a knife edge; few trust the government. Everything is a bit dodgy. Their solution is to dance in the streets and party, eat, drink and be merry for tomorrow..........? They really have got it right. But something happened a few nights ago and it keeps coming back to haunt me.

We were walking back, late at night, and came across an old gentleman looking like an archetypal university professor. He stopped us and, at first, I thought he must have heard us talking. Maybe he wanted to chat. So many people have waylaid us, wanting to talk, practise their English, ask us questions. It then slowly dawned on me, he was begging. We were covered in embarrassment and he was too. It was painful and humiliating and so surreal. He had a three-piece suit on and a tie. He was my father's generation with that endearing old-fashioned politeness. It was no worse than a homeless man begging but somehow, it was. A society collapsing in on itself. We walked home thinking how much it must have cost him to beg, the loss of honour, his loss of respect. This old gentleman stripped down to his outstretched hand.

So, there you have it dearest ones, I just wanted to share it with you.

With love,

Angie

to:	family and friends
from:	Joyful Traveller
subject:	Argentina - Wild horses with a wild daughter on the Argentinian Pampas.

These group emails are almost as bad as those ghastly round-robin Christmas letters, aren't they? The ones where everyone is so perfect. Children achieving so much, new cars and expensive holidays. But today, I'm feeling a bit homesick so I thought I'd write to you.

Said goodbye to Nessie this morning, on her way back home to start her TEFL course. She's been a complete joy, as usual, except for the little encounter she had with horses and no regard for her (possibly neurotic) mother's feelings......

We were on a ranch about a hundred miles outside Buenos Aires. Kenneth was happily left behind, savouring the peace and quiet. I had visions of nice mild-mannered horses, teachers in smart riding breeches - and helmets, unquestionably compulsory.

We arrived and all I could see were these wild-looking Argentinian horses. Great big things with fiery eyes and snorting noses and not an instructor in sight.

We rarely shout at each other, but that all changed.

To begin with, I started to reason with her. This did not make a blind bit of difference. I then cried; big sobs rattled in my throat. Still, she would not give in. The problem was the helmet, or the lack of it. They just didn't have any, none on the whole wretched ranch.

Two guests from Chile, super fit, muscular types, overheard me getting hysterical. It was impossible not to hear us as by now, I had visions of Nessie falling off on her head and being paralysed for life.

They informed me in a smirky, somewhat condescending manner,

"Do not worry, I am sure your daughter is a brilliant horsewoman, she looks like one", and then surveyed me from top to bottom in an unkind sort of way. I could tell they were thinking,

"Well, you certainly don't".

The Chileans could smell my fear and my abiding dislike and mistrust of horses. Sensing this, they decided they disliked me as well. Mind you, I'm a bit like that with dogs, can never understand people who don't like dogs.

So, I stood there shaking with resentment and anger. For two pins I would have slapped them hard and told them they were fools and irresponsible and reckless. I felt utterly powerless. It would be impossible to change our plans, there was nowhere to go.

I had to accept that Nessie would ride these crazy horses without a helmet. In my desperate moments I did think about locking her in the bathroom but she would have screamed so loudly, I'd have been had up for child abuse.

I tried so hard not to watch her while she was riding. I would go walking in the opposite direction, but one day there she was galloping over a field, a scrubby, uneven field. She could have been in some wretched shampoo advert. Long, wavy sun-streaked hair fanning out behind her, and a look of sheer joy on her lovely face.

I would walk and swim surrounded by a vast array of animals; lamas, wild pigs, untethered horses, hummingbirds and parrots - all the while praying she wouldn't fall off the crazy horse. My prayers were answered.

In a few days' time we fly down to the most southerly city in the world, Ushuaia. From there we travel by ship for a week around Argentina and the Chilean fjords. Unfortunately, I just have to look at a boat and I start to turn green!

Have bought five pairs of sandals; none of them fit me but they're lovely to look at.

My Spanish is still non-existent: how can I be so bad at something?

With love,

Angie

to: family and friends

from: Joyful Traveller

subject: Ushuaia, Argentina - The End of The World

Dear Ones,

We are in the world's most southerly city, the last one before you reach the Antarctic, and it feels just like that. The End of the World is the nickname for Ushuaia. A very odd place. As usual, we are not in any swanky hotel although I doubt they have any here. We're staying in a small, 'keenly-priced' (The Scotsman's expression, not mine), guest house. Situated outside the town, down lots of unpaved side streets and up an unlit, dark, foreboding track.

This area is a run-down, grubby, creepy place scattered with houses that look like childrens' dens. Many are held together with an odd assortment of materials; bits of piping, corrugated iron, lumps of hardboard - all add to the jumble of neglected shacks. Newspapers are tacked to the inside of windows, according to Kenneth, they act as insulation. Tin roofs sit precariously on top. A strong wind might unleash them sending them off into the sky. Random dwellings appear, town planning hasn't ever seen the light of day. It's a harsh, jumbled mess and among this mess are endless packs of dogs. They bark all night and snarl in the daytime.

In the town there are a few tourists - the nerdy types in anoraks and walking boots.

Our ship has come in! Last night, there she was, in the harbour. Kenneth has reverted to his lost childhood. He keeps chortling and rubbing his hands together with glee. I cannot understand all the fuss, but will wait and see.

With love,

Angie

Dearests.

Here we are on the boat. It's full of very earnest types who have been down to the Antarctic. A nice bunch of people. I don't imagine there will be much karaoke or wild drinking on board this vessel.

Leaving the guest house this morning I learnt something I'd rather wish I hadn't. For a neurotic with a wild imagination, it wasn't the best way to start the day.

We had been walking around Ushuaia for several days. Often coming across packs of dogs. Sometimes friendly, sometimes suspicious and sometimes very scary. Kenneth and I stupidly believe we have 'a way with dogs' so when these gangs approached us, I would assume the manner of Barbara Woodhouse. I became her. Do you remember her? I would watch her television programme enthralled as she dealt with the most difficult of dogs. She was magnificent. A very proper, loud, commanding dog expert. She only had to say one word, give one of her terrifying looks and dogs would be putty in her hands. I'd perfected my Barbara Woodhouse manner years ago. Now was the time to put it to use.

When these dogs approached, I would give commands and shake the walking stick, I'd bought in the town, vowing it would come in handy. The dogs would slink off. They had met their match.

At breakfast time, presiding over the toast and cereals was the owner, a Brazilian lady who had entranced each of her guests with her beauty and fabulous figure.

She would sail into the breakfast room. You could hear her before she arrived. Numerous amounts of jangling gold bracelets, dangling earrings that moved in time with her magnificent bosoms. These were always displayed in tight low-cut tee shirts.

She would smile an awful lot of the time and there behind her deep red lipstick were huge amounts of gleaming gnashers.

She asked me if we had found everything satisfactory. I replied that everything had been fine apart from the packs of roaming dogs which we had to navigate through each day. Something that had troubled us a little.

In a split second, completely unabashed, she hauled up her flouncy skirt and pulled up her tee-shirt. There amongst the bosoms was the most horrific scar. She pointed out the length of it. From her chest to just below her knee. A thick blue-black imprint on that wonderful body.

"I was attacked by one of them"

"One what?" I asked, aghast as I stared at the deep, vicious scar.

"One of those dogs".

At that moment I didn't know what to do. On one hand I felt so sorry for her, on the other I wanted to scream at her. Why hadn't she warned us? She looked at me with a mixture of shame and defiance, turned and sashayed away. I suppose it would have been bad for business.

I'm now thinking of one encounter with a particularly bad-tempered animal on our last night. A ragged, angry animal whose ribs stuck out at the sides, with a belly dragging almost to the floor. We locked eyes. The creature might have seen a look of compassion mixed with a fighting spirit. Whatever he had spied in my expression, he slunk away. We'd had, a lucky escape.

I'm a hideous sailor. We haven't even moved, and my stomach is sinking. No one is in the computer room, all of the passengers are out on deck being very serious. Better get some fresh air while I can.

Beware of wild dogs.

With love,

Angie

to: **family and friends**

from: **Joyful Traveller**

subject: **Argentina to Chile - Line-dancing, inquisitive penguins and overexcited cockroaches**

Hello You Lovely Ones,

Here we are on the boat and my worst fears have not been realised …. yet. Haven't thrown up, almost did - but not quite. It's strange how the body gets acquainted with and adapts to various conditions. When we leave the boat, we miss the perpetual motion and need to recover our 'land legs'.

It's a very sedate affair. Lots of serious-minded individuals, ecologists, environmentalists and fanatic whale-watchers. An agreeable lot of people making their way from the very bottom of Argentina to the port of Valparaiso in Chile.

The most exciting thing on offer in the evenings is a line-dancing class. That, too, was quite a staid affair. Us middle-aged lot trying to get our feet to match the moves, in time to the music. I placed myself at the back of the class hoping it would allow me to watch the other dancers and not look like a complete twit. Being new to this, I didn't realise you have to pivot round. Now there I was positioned at the front and making a complete dog's dinner of it. With an exaggerated whisper one elderly lady behind me hissed,

"Well dear, you haven't been practicing, have you?"

Think I might give line-dancing a miss.  *practising*

The melting of the glaciers is terrifying. Terrifying to watch great chucks power their way down to the sea. I just can't think about it at the moment. What a coward I am and how selfish my generation has been and continues to be. I will have to take action but, for now, I'm being self-centred, materialistic and ignorant. Promising myself I will have to fight for our planet soon, before it becomes all too late.

We made a stop at a penguin colony. Not many of the passengers fancied lurching into the small boats which ferried us over the angry waves to the shore. The possibility of being close to these birds was irresistible although while on this small vessel I was having second thoughts. It was a frantic ride to get to the shore, our stomachs and hearts hung in the air.

A short bus ride later and we reached the colony. At the entrance, it was all rather draconian but extremely well organised, which I was so thankful for. The entrance fee helped with the upkeep of the coast and research into the habits of the colony. The safety and freedom of the penguins was paramount. The guide made it startlingly clear that the rules had to be obeyed.

Narrow paths zig-zagged down to the shore, roped off from the land; there could be no wavering from the trail. Voices had to be kept to a whisper, groups of people were discouraged. Visitors broke off into pairs. Photography and videoing were permitted as long as it didn't interfere with the penguins' activities.

I think our little group thought we'd see a few penguins in the far distance, if we were lucky, so we trundled off. After five minutes of walking carefully along the paths it happened.

One popped out of the dunes and waddled over to us, looking like a bossy waiter. His friends followed. As we continued to walk yet more penguins appeared and what happened next was quite magical. Lots of little dramas were being played out right in front of our eyes. It took on the feel of a comedy show. Penguins who seemed devoid of a set of brakes came crashing into each other as they spotted a friend. Like dominos, they would fall over and then get up with a surprised look about them. The tubby ones would try and jump over rocks waiting earnestly, trying to muster up some courage. Often, they would not make it and have to scramble up a rock in a most ungainly manner, all embarrassed and a little flustered. There seemed to be hundreds of penguins going about their everyday business, totally oblivious to us humans.

I was joined on the path by three feathered companions and we waddled along together. Sometimes we would all stop and they would look at me. Their heads turning from side to side, wondering what sort of creature I could possibly be. Then off we'd go again, chests expanded, little feet marching towards the sea.

As they entered the sea all the awkwardness, the bumbling ways, disappeared. In the ocean they were streamline, beautiful, elegant and graceful.

Streamlined

I think I'll tell you about an encounter with some creepy crawlies. Hope you are not reading this as you munch on your breakfast, it could put you off it.

We stopped again along the way. The boat discharged its passengers – again, all anoraks and sturdy walking boots. It was a small fishing town with an excited market plonked in the middle of the settlement; vibrant, loud, teeming with swarms of people milling around the numerous fish counters. Where does all this fish come from? Who eats it all? Rows upon rows of hundreds of fish. Outlandish looking fish, showy-off fish, fish taken from scary fairy tales. All the time, the robust lady fish sellers with the arms of wrestlers were splashing grubby looking water over their wares. It was chaotic and fierce and exhilarating. Huge vats of bubbling concoctions whose cooks manhandled ladles so large you could paddle a boat with them. Enticing smells hanging in the air muddled with the pungent smell of raw fish.

We were hungry. Both the Scotsman and I have the digestive constitutions of an ox and believe that if the food is local and thoroughly cooked, we'd not encounter the dreaded tummy bugs so many travellers fear.

A cheerful young chap ushered us into a plastic booth, the type that is easy to wash down but makes your bottom slide around. No menus appeared but what did arrive in a matter of moments was a steaming plate of deliciousness. It was so delicious I failed to notice what was behind Kenneth's head for a few moments. A mixture of fish and rice, chili and spices had to be focussed on, every bite bringing exquisite pleasure.

Then I saw them. At first, I was not sure what I was looking at. They appeared to be waving at me. I peered, almost reluctantly, not wanting to take my attention away from the scrumptious food. They scurried around just inches away from Kenneth's head. Now more of them arrived, roaming around the back of the seat. Huge black cockroaches had gathered, notifying each other of the possibility of food.

Kenneth sensed I was staring at him and as he lifted his head, he too, had a rather startled expression on his face, one he quickly tried hard to hide. Of course, they were behind me too. I jumped up and the waiter appeared. In agitation I pointed to the army of black things streaming around the back of my seat and to the opposing army opposite me. Kenneth had stayed firmly in his seat continuing to relish his plate of food.

The young man giggled and did a bit of flicking with his grimy cloth. A cluster of these nasties jumped off and landed on our table. Overturned now, their frantic efforts to right themselves were watched with what seemed like amusement by the waiter and the other diners sat near to us. He swept them aside with the back of his hand and pointed to my seat.

I took my seat, sitting upright making sure I wasn't touching the back of the seat and then focused my gaze upon my plate; after all the food was so mouth wateringly delicious, I couldn't let it go to waste.

With love,

Angie

to: family and friends

from: Joyful Traveller

subject: Valparaiso and Santiago. Chile -
When our ship came in

It was a fairy-tale scene as we slowly chugged into Valparaiso harbour. Early morning mist swirled around the many hills. Brightly coloured houses tumbled down the streets, lights peering out of the windows. We watched a magical kingdom come into sight and became enchanted.

The nearer we drew towards the port the clearer I could see the hills. Each one seemed to have two strange contraptions slowly snaking their way up and down. I had been reading about the funiculars, cable-driven rail carts and here they were. Wonderful ways of keeping the population moving up and down those steep slopes. They were introduced in the 1880's, still surviving and a vital part of this city.

It's a little rough around the edges, this captivating place, which probably contributes to its charm. It's like a badly dressed lady who has seen better days. In the words of the great and famous Chilean poet, Pablo Neruda, he describes Valparaiso,

"Never did you have time to dress yourself".

The houses are often dilapidated. Scuffed edges and roof tops with missing tiles. Balconies sway in the wind. They seem to stay up but look as though a more forceful wind could blow them away. The streets are cobbled and a threat to any footwear with heels. Palm trees are held up with twisting, thick, rope-like bougainvillea and vines.

Everywhere seems to display some decoration. Glorious graffiti which could stand happily alongside fine art in a museum. The talent spills out onto the pavement. Every wall, side of building, paving stones - anywhere a paint brush might fit is covered with fabulous art. Often political, humorous, coupled with charming portraits of flowers.

Amongst this poetic and wonderful mess are the people we met. Warm hearted, kind and just a lovely lot. Proud of their city and keen to transfer their enthusiasm to anyone willing to listen.

Pablo Neruda, who wrote beautiful poetry, lived here. He wanted an eyrie somewhere high above the city, somewhere which embodied his personality. He was a womaniser, an extrovert, a bon viveur. A huge personality who needed a bolt hole; his house reflects this. We visited it a few days ago and I am still remembering little slices of it. Strange ornaments, some clutter between the breath-taking views over the port and out to sea. I wondered if the sea glistens all year round.

Stray dogs pick a person they find appealing and like to stay as close to them as possible, acting a little like an enthusiastic canine tour guide. We were chosen by two scabby mongrels who I dreamt of taking back home. Clever dogs who all seem to get along with each other. Locals leave food out and there are lots of water bowls scattered around the city. The dogs somehow blend in wonderfully well. No pedigrees here, more kind-natured ruffians. This is their city, and they seem just as proud of it as their human counterparts.

The amazing funicular railways, all twenty-two of them, are still going strong. It was the British and the German communities who lived high up in the hills, where the air was fresh, who built the first one in 1883. They linked the business part of the city down below to their posh homes up in the hills. Two cars move up and down the steep hillsides in opposite directions. They are painted wood and metal cabins mounted on platforms that are attached to wheels.

We were just about to board one of the funiculars when the operator stopped us. He must have heard us talking and with much enthusiasm, drew us into his controller cubby-hole. He was bursting with pride as he showed off the controls. Every nut, bolt and piece of machinery gleamed. The brass shone like sunshine and he announced,

"British, a British made, you British, this is yours".

He insisted we take photographs especially of the British wrought-iron stamp which he proudly polished with much vigour in front of us. As we boarded the passenger compartment, he emerged from his post wildly waving at us, shouting his best wishes. The other passengers gazed at us, maybe wondering if we were important people.

We arrived in Santiago and immediately felt at home, more relaxed. Gentler than Valparaiso; like a well-behaved aunt. The walls of buildings too are painted, but in a more sophisticated manner. Large squares appear as if by magic tempting the visitor to sit and just be. Trees are everywhere casting shade and filling the streets with dappled shadows in the warm light.

This country is nestled amongst one of the world's largest mountain ranges, one of the driest deserts and one of the largest oceans.

The people we meet are exceptionally helpful and gracious, all wanting to show-off their city in its best light. Opening a map acted like a beacon, it proved to be a great way to meet locals. Sitting on a bus poring over our map, a young woman asked us where we were going. We told her and she implied that she, too, was going there. We trooped off the bus together and she pointed to the street we needed. We said goodbye and thanked her. Walking up the hill I turned around and saw she was back at the bus stop, waiting for another bus. I realised then that she had got off the bus expressly to show us where to go.

Delicious food here, especially the empanadas. A bit like a Cornish pasty stuffed with assorted fillings and always oozing plenty of cheese. Raw fish which melts in the mouth marinated with lavish amounts of herbs and spices, swimming in fresh lemon juice. Hearty beef stews with potatoes, pumpkins and corn noodles. Scrumptiously smelling sausages plonked into fresh white bread.

We're off to get some lunch.

"Kenneth, I think I will have a salad today", but it is the empanadas that always seem to win, after all, I think that might be the national dish.

With love,

Angie

to: family and friends

from: Joyful Traveller

subject: Vrindavan India. 2008 - Hope and Hare Krishna

Dear Ones,

So, this is our plan. Susie, my sister, has already started teaching here. This came about because her best friend is a Hare Krishna devotee, who lives in the same town in Italy as Susie does. A gorgeous soul; a softly spoken, highly artistic, talented American from the mid-West. While walking along a road she encountered the man she would marry, an Italian born Hare Krishna follower. It was as simple as that. Their eyes met and, as they say, the rest is history. She knew that India, and especially the Hare Krishna school here in Vrindavan, would steal Susie's heart, and it has.

I plan to tag along for a few days then leave to visit Nessie in the Himalayas. On my return, Susie will come hotel-inspecting with me to Rajasthan. She will have deserved a well-earned rest and a bit of an adventure.

Susie is a believer in past lives she thinks that she must have been here before, if you saw her, you would think so too.

She somehow fits in here perfectly. Susie is fine boned - unlike me - and sort of wafts around while I lumber along beside her. She covers her head in fine voile scarves and could easily be mistaken for a pale-faced lady of noble birth. The intense heat only appears to make her face seem a little damp; with me, I continually feel sweat trickling down my back, my face permanently dripping. Glasses steam up and my patience leaves me.

We walk past open sewers on our way to the school and watch pigs scavenging in the rubbish, while all forms of human life are played out on the streets.

Vrindavan is believed to be the place where Lord Krishna spent his younger days frolicking with Radha. It is a holy place for Hindus, and some believe if you die here you will be free from the reincarnation cycle. Another name for this place is The City of Widows.

Is this what brings the hoards of widows here?

There are thought to be over 20,000 of these white clad women. They come seeking peace and salvation. Some are thought to be lured here by their children and then abandoned. Some are simply alone in the world. Others are banished by their husbands' families preventing them from inheriting property. Groups of them gather outside the numerous temples and beg. These are mostly broken women. Women who, to keep starvation from the door, offer prayers and chanting each morning and evening for many long hours in return for a cup of rice from the local temples. Ashrams set up by various NGO's are full and often overcrowded.

Catching sight of them at dawn or when the sun is setting can take your breath away. Like lost spirits drifting by, invisible and forsaken. In some sections of society a widow is considered to be an omen of bad luck, even her shadow is thought to be contaminated.

I try my best not to catch their eye but if I do my heart sinks and the misery of this last chapter of their lives is palpable. I can almost taste it, sour and rotten.

But then there is the school where Susie has been teaching where grace and kindness seems to surround everything and everyone.

I remember with great fondness the ardent followers of Krishna who would parade up and down London's Oxford Street. Saffron garments flowing, tambourines, bells, drums and with great happiness snaking their way through the often miserable and annoyed pedestrians. And here I was, helping out in a Hare Krishna school in India.

The devotee in charge wears saffron coloured robes with a shaved head apart from a piece of hair resembling a little tail which falls down the back of his head. All devotees have this, a shikha. At the point of death, Krishna will pull the soul from the topmost chakra which is on the head under this tuft of hair. It also attracts cosmic energy, said to impart enlightenment.

This man is exceptionally handsome with a strong Italian accent which only adds to his charisma. He could have stepped out of a page of a Vogue magazine - or one of those models who advertises designer aftershave lotions - turns out he was. His life was damaged and unfulfilled and one day he found Krishna. This extraordinary man then founded, and now runs, this school for hundreds of desperately poor children.

The school educates over 1,500 girls who, without his vision, would have little, if any, education. Every girl wears a uniform, every uniform is pristine. Long black hair tied up into plaits or ponytails. Eager faces which seem to have a smile permanently placed there.

The school exudes feelings of hope and achievement. A sense of purpose and gratefulness pervades every corner. Education is the precious jewel these children have been given.

Lunchtime and everyone sits on the floor. We are served rice, lentils, chapatis and a strange yellow coloured vegetable. This is all presented on a large banana leaf. I try to eat with my hands, my left hand, and fail wretchedly. Turmeric stains will not wash out of my white trousers but I don't care. The noise and laughter and the joy are contagious.

The food is delicious, and I don't miss the lack of onions, garlic, or mushrooms. These are ingredients which are thought to heat up the brain and are not permitted along with caffeine and alcohol.

They are a jolly bunch. At the temple last night watching the devotees whirling around with lots of jumping up and down, I felt a little envious. One of the teachings is to be as happy as you can possibly manage, maybe that's why they handle the hardship here.

Yesterday was a festival and while walking through a temple a large group of people approached Susie and I and asked if we would take their photograph. They meant they wanted to take our photo with all of them in it. Suddenly, it turned into a frenzied scene. From almost every corner of the temple more and more people appeared and crowded in, happy and excited. In the end Susie and I had to prise ourselves away and bolt for the exit, leaving the crowd waving and asking for more photos. It was all so joyous.

I leave for the north soon. I'm so very proud of my sister. At times I can imagine her staying here, making it her home. Selfishly, I won't let myself think about that for too long. She has a natural affinity with the children, the staff, with everything here. Vrindavan is a hard, unforgiving place.

Yesterday, we visited the home of one of the schoolgirls who Susie sponsors. She is a beautiful teenager. Her uniform is spotless. She is diligent, enthusiastic, full of life, her greatest desire is to continue with her education. Her home was in a filthy compound. We had to struggle over the foul-smelling stream which runs along the entrance, brandishing our sun umbrellas at the bad-tempered, filth-covered pigs that were staggering in and out of the dark evil water. There was her home, a structure made out of bundles of sticks covered in black plastic. A dirt floor and various iron beds sat close to each other. The kitchen was a fire pit outside. I didn't see any evidence of a toilet.

I came away thinking of the beautiful man and all the countless other people all beavering away at the school. The teachers, assistants, cleaners, administrators, cooks and fundraisers. It was this band of amazing souls who had made it possible, giving hundreds of young girls the chance of an education, which in turn could change and enrich their lives.

A reward in heaven? and though I know followers of Hare Krishna do not believe in a heaven, for now, their reward is here on earth - watching young lives being transformed.

With love,

Angie

Finally, the monkey dropped my bag and made off with the sweets, his red bottom bobbing up and down through the crowded alleyway.

The children gathered expectantly around me. I gave them what I thought was a generous reward, it seemed like a generous sum but they were not pleased with it. They wanted, and expected, more. That is when it suddenly dawned on me, the penny dropped. I had been scammed by a bunch of children, and a well-trained monkey. Admiring their tenacity and entrepreneurial skills I dug into my bag, now covered with slimy monkey goo, and handed over more cash. They smiled and nonchalantly wandered off - probably in search of their next unsuspecting victim.

I must go now and find something to eat. It's almost lunchtime and my tummy is rumbling. The dogs are now sprawled out on the street, unmoving, saving their precious energy until the sun sets. Not so the monkey family who I spy as I peer through the grubby windows of the Internet café. They're busy picking fleas from each other with a constant eye out for another victim. Today, there will be no treasures from me. I have cleverly constructed a belt which is wound around my waist inside my clothes with my precious possessions jammed into a small bag that is wedged in there. They can't possibly get to it...... can they?

With love,

Angie.

Written on the side of my box of breakfast cereal this morning:

> 'New European Muesli will help purify the blood, add vigour to your day, aid poorly digestion, and keep brain in tip-top condition should you be wanting a beneficially start to the day's work'.

Doesn't seem to have helped me much with the old brain cells...... but I'm hopeful.

I left Vrindavan, it was a bit of a relief to get to Delhi where I am staying tonight.

Indian train journeys are like no others. I wandered through various carriages seeing how cheerful and accommodating everyone was. When there are no seats or a place to sit on the floor, the luggage racks come in handy. One fellow was eating a curry balanced on a luggage rack, struggling to get food into his mouth as he smiled at me as I walked by. Towards the back of the train dozens of passengers who didn't manage to actually get inside the train were clinging onto the doors, squashed together, shouting up to others who were hugging the roof.

So many trees in Delhi and where there's any bit of scrubby greenery there's sure to be a cricket match in full flow. Few open sewers unlike Vrindavan - and delicious coffee at the Internet café where I am sitting right now. Booked a very cheap hotel which informs guests, "not to be checking in until 8pm at the earliest". Well, it's only for the night, um…

Tomorrow, I fly to Kullu, in the foothills of the Himalayas, to meet Nessie who has been living in a community there for the last eight months. I'm excited, a little apprehensive and keep repeating to myself, "Love is letting go".

It was her decision to stay there, to embrace the teachings, to become part of this community. I must make sure I don't let her down. I have to become open and accepting and leave all my prejudices and things I might have heard about religious sects and ashrams at the entrance to this place.

Wish me luck.

With love,

Angie

to: family and friends

from: Joyful Traveller

subject: Delhi India - An Indian 'Budget' Hotel

Hi Everyone,

An Indian 'Budget Hotel' is not an experience for the faint-hearted, so long as you don't need to sleep it's almost bearable. I was going to go for the dormitory option - thought the Scotsman would be proud of me – and on reflection, that might have been a better option than my 'Premier Room'.

I had a very early start in the morning so I asked the ageing chap behind the counter if I could have a wake-up call. He continued to pick his few remaining teeth furiously throughout our encounter. He looked bemused and cheerful all at the same time, then earnestly assured me I would wake up on time. I have always had a dread of sleeping through my alarm but this time, as it turned out, I didn't need to worry.

Some rather suspicious looking bugs were careering around the room. So, I showered, then coated my entire body in copious amounts of insect repellent cream. I pulled back the greying bedspread to find two grubby looking pillowcases and no sheets. The mattress was covered in stains that all seemed to merge into one another, creating a kaleidoscope of colour. For a fleeting moment of horror I let myself imagine what gruesome creatures would be nestling in there. With no such luxury as a telephone in this room, I pulled myself together, flung on my clothes and waddled downstairs forgetting I was covered in heavy duty cream. My clothes were now clinging to me. This is not a good look - especially in a cheap hotel. I resembled someone who had taken part in a weird wet tee-shirt competition. The elderly man, now raising an eyebrow behind the desk, found it hard to take his eyes off my protruding breasts. He even stopped picking his teeth.

Finally, the sheets arrived and I was left to make the bed. The sheets were made of the thinnest of thin material, almost translucent and peppered with little holes. Exhausted, I crept into bed refusing to think of all the unwashed bodies that might have used these sheets and not at all convinced they had ever been anywhere near a laundry.

I was now faced with two choices - but first, a word about Indian electrics in Budget Hotels. You are given a key which is supposed to fit into some very dodgy-looking electrical socket that should be attached to the wall. It is not attached to the wall, it is precariously hanging off it, dangling in the breeze. The key operates both the air-conditioning system and the lights, take the key out and no air-conditioning and no lights. Decide I'll put on my eyeshades to stop the glare of the almost stadium-like lighting and keep the air-conditioning on. This doesn't last long. As I lie in bed, I become convinced that I shall be bodily lifted out of the room by the power of the air-conditioner and I can feel my face starting to freeze over. I'm sure I am going to die of frostbite.

I turn the blaster off and now hear Indian television reverberating all around the room. To make matters worse, the man in the next-door bathroom must have a problem, possibly induced by a very hot and indigestible curry. The sounds emanating through the paper-thin walls are extremely forceful. I try my best to shut out this noise but as I do another sound becomes audible.

Have you ever had to share a bedroom with a cricket? I can only describe it as a form of excruciating torture. It starts off quite softly and then gathers momentum. Just when you think you will go crazy, the noise stops. You are then lulled into a false sense of security believing, foolishly, that he/she/it has gone to sleep, got fed up, developed a sore throat … but not for long. It starts all over again. I try desperately to kill it and end up using my one and only towel which had fallen on the bathroom floor. Plumbing in Budget Hotels leaves a lot to be desired. The floor still swims with my old shower water, scummy and grey, nicely matching everything else in this place. I now attack the bedroom walls. Flinging the sodden towel where I think this infuriating insect might be, I miss every time. Slink back into bed, close my eyes, willing my brain not to hear the incessant sound.

It's the dead of night now and I start to hear a voice, getting louder and louder. I peer through my spy hole and there, parading up and down the corridor, is this man. At first, I think I still might be dreaming, John Travolta in my corridor. White suit and slicked black hair, he's showing off his new mobile phone. He continues to shout into it even though it's on loudspeaker. The sound of the equally hysterical person on the other end of the line bounces off the walls. I am now beside myself with rage and scream through my door telling this voice to, "SHUT UP".

Unbelievably, it all goes quiet - suspiciously so. I'm peering through the spy hole and can see nothing. I return to bed then decide to check the lock on my door and to my horror realise that it doesn't actually work. It's now 3.30 in the morning. The insect repellent cream has given up on the buzzy, biting insects. I'm dripping with sweat, scratching my skin to pieces and starting to hallucinate, believing some mad mobile-wielding lunatic is outside my door trying to get in. I decided I needed some sort of barricade so I drag the heaviest piece of furniture I can find across the room and pile it by the door. I collapse back onto the bed.

The next thing I know I'm being woken by a furious banging on my door, my alarm call. I sit bolt upright and have no idea where on earth I am. Slivers of panic start to crawl up my spine. I take a couple of strangled breaths and remember but.... not quick enough. I go to put the key into the power socket, stub my toe so badly on the piled-up furniture that I collapse back onto the bed clutching my toe which I now believe might be broken. The chap next door sounds as though he's about to take off, the cricket has been practicing again and his voice is stronger than ever and the blaring sound of Indian television is still managing to seep through the walls. I lie alongside my wet towel and vow with all my heart that:

I SHALL NEVER STAY IN AN INDIAN BUDGET HOTEL EVER AGAIN, EVER.

With love,

Angie

to:　　　family and friends

from:　　Joyful Traveller

subject:　Kullu, India - A very special being

I'm in the foothills of the Himalayas, the Valley of the Gods, and that just about sums it up.

Nessie is flourishing. Radiant and loving life, studying, hiking, finding faith and a spiritual path. It was the most wonderful of reunions. There she was clutching a bunch of flowers and a face lit up with glee, as I and the rest of the passengers, most of whom had turned an odd shade of green - including the crew, staggered off the aircraft.

It was a small plane, rather like one of those wooden aeroplanes children would build from scratch. I think the material was called balsa wood with a tube of glue thrown in. Never quite knowing if all the bits would fit, but you carried on regardless - just like the flight from Delhi.

We lurched frantically from side to side and often the plane would suddenly drop in height prompting huge gasps of breath and chanting of prayers by fellow passengers. I would look up to the panel above my head and be surprised that the oxygen masks hadn't come tumbling down.

I should have been more prepared at check-in, the ground staff looked troubled. Two of them sitting on their stools with furrowed brows.

"Madam, we cannot do check-ins yet".

"Oh, why not, I thought the plane is due to depart in under an hour?".

"Madam, we have to monitor the weather".

"Why? The weather looks very settled here".

"Ah yes, but not near the mountains. It is a difficult airport to land in", said as they exchanged knowing glances between themselves.

"What do you mean?"

And with my last question they both waved me away. That fascinating, almost unique Indian motion, a sort of flick of the wrist, which is often employed when they have had enough, are bored or, in this case, just can't answer the question. I was dismissed.

Happily, I made it here and now I'm sitting surrounded by an assortment of lavatory paper, boxes of tissues, packs of pan scourers, sacks full of Jiffy mops and other bits of cleaning and household paraphernalia. In the corner, is one rather lonely, dusty computer which I am using. I dare not look up, if I catch the eye of the delightful owner I will never get this finished. We have already talked for over an hour, mostly about the meaning of life. He seems, like many people here, to understand it, that wonderful knowledge and understanding of life and death - and all the bits in between.

India, rural India. This is no ashram set in lush green mountains away from the frenetic pace of life. Guru Swami Ji wanted it to be accessible, not hidden away, part of the community, so it's on a busy, dusty main road.

Cars driven at a frenetic pace, followed by brightly painted lorries stuffed with every conceivable object you could imagine; fridges, lamp shades, crates of tomatoes, small cars, bikes, mattresses, chickens, cauliflowers, beds and hairdryers - all manically piled up to the sky. These vehicles are determined to overtake anything that gets it their way. Then motorbikes appear. The driver always wears a crash helmet while the rest of the family, often consisting of a wife with a tiny baby strapped to her plus a couple or more children perched on the back seldom wear helmets. Tuk-tuks and cows bring up the rear. The tuk-tuks are often crammed to the brim with an assortment of passengers hanging on for dear life while the death-defying driver navigates the madness. Buses the same, rusted and patched up until there is more rust that metal holding them all together. The cows are sometimes not the gentle bovine creatures you imagine them to be, wandering the streets of India. Some are bulls whose owners have abandoned them. They are sharp-eyed and bad-tempered. Negotiating the dust, the rubbish piled high, animal excrement, angry cows as well as the constant stream of traffic is something of a challenge every day.

I've been here for over a week now and starting to feel like part of the community. I open my door each morning, braving the noise. Every driver appears to have his hand permanently pressed on the vehicle's horn - even if there is nothing in front of him. Maybe they're just hedging their bets. I'm getting to know most of the shopkeepers by name. I know what day the rubbish is collected and what television programmes my neighbours listen to, at ear shattering volume. The ashram folk live cheek by jowl with the locals. I can see right into my neighbour's bathroom. Once you get used to the dust, which the shopkeepers obligingly wipe away from every purchase you make, the non-existent pavements, the potholes, showers of miserable tepid little dribbles, it is quite magical.

On the roads ancient ladies are bent double by the huge loads they carry on their backs. Bundles of sticks and green palms obliterate their faces - worn and lined like an elephant's skin while bright, dancing eyes peer out beneath. They carry knurled wooden walking sticks. Their clothes are layered and rugs are often wrapped around their middles.

In the markets, tall mounds of garlic, limes and ginger are displayed in a precarious fashion while the lady vendors sit under tatty umbrellas. Hot red chillies match the colour of the saris that pass by.

Girls in their school uniforms of crisp white blouses and blue and green tartan kilts look somehow incongruous. Their ponytails and pigtails are immaculate. They laugh and are so very polite and interested - just delightful.

It's become a habit every night to check for scorpions that might have taken a fancy to my bedding - often my shoes. Then the spiders that lurk around the toilet seat. I'm getting a little weary of curry at every meal. Few fresh salads and all vegetables are boiled to within an inch of their lives, everything is coated in ghee or lashing of oil. The bread is delicious though. Tibetan bread, heavy and dense to keep out the cold in winter and to stop the tummy from rumbling. I've become a vegetarian and not a drop of alcohol has passed my lips since I staggered off the aeroplane.

The rains came last week. The streets were awash with mud. I would jump and run from the edge of one gigantic pool of water to another. Amongst all this are the devotees, the Sharms as they are called. A wonderful and fascinating group of people. Artists, writers, film makers, professors, scientists, mathematicians. They have come from all over the world and this is where they have decided to live, to make this place their home and all because there is the most extraordinary being here.

You enter another realm when you are in the presence of Swami Ji. I've been able to feel that bliss which I have hardly ever experienced before, the kind of joy I felt after giving birth to my children.

Swami calls it Pure, Unchanging, Free Forever. Meditating on that spiritual level, getting a glimpse of God Consciousness, of The Oneness where there is no form, no words, just pure space and a glimpse of heaven. I have experienced being in the presence of a realised being and I've never felt more joy or peace.

And now there's a long queue of eager school children behind my seat, waiting patiently to use the only computer in the village.

With love,

Angie

This was the scene. I was sat in a taxi outside Delhi International airport at 2.30am this morning. My sister, ashen-faced and weak, summons up enough energy to plead with me.

"You will come home with us now please, please. You can't go off travelling around India on your own".

She has caught typhoid and is very, very poorly.

Nessie sits there all 22 years of her. An old soul, one that has been here before, one that fights her battles and now wants to fight for her mother. She sits next to me and has that look I know so well. She was born with that look, a look that somehow says, "I'm not afraid of anything, so don't stop me" and she's trying with all her might to transfer it to me.

She turns and with a look of wilful promise and a steely voice says:

"Ma if you don't stay and do this inspecting I will never, ever again have any respect for you".

She knows how to turn the screw, she knows where my weak spot is, she knows her power and she loves me deeply. This brave, strong, inspiring girl is showing me the courage I might have.

So, they leave me, sitting in a taxi in the middle of the night outside Delhi International airport.

The taxi driver throughout these exchanges has been forming his own ideas. He has sat patiently waiting, desperate to impart some knowledge only he would know and now he looks with a mixture of pity and horror at me. There's this woman sat in the back of his taxi in the middle of the night with nowhere to go.

"These children of ours, so troubling Madam".

"Yes, you could say that".

I now wonder what on earth I was thinking of. Here I am all alone in the middle of the night but with India at my feet.

"Do you know of anywhere I could get a room for tonight?"

"Madam, oh yes, the YMCA always have rooms, especially for someone in your predicament"

So, he takes me to the YMCA and yes, they have a room and not only that, they give me Heinz tomato soup followed by strawberry Angel Delight and I'm so happy. I do a little jig around my room and fall into a deep dreamy sleep which features elephants and palaces and Maharajas - and that feeling of only having one life here as we know it, enters my very soul.

More to come my darlings.

With love,

Angie

to: family and friends

from: Joyful Traveller

subject: India, Jaipur - Taking tea in style

My first assignment as a hotel inspector in Rajasthan, and I end up taking tea with royalty.

93 years old and still feisty. An inspiring, totally enchanting individual. Her family has converted one of their homes into the lovely hotel where I am staying.

She holds court, in this she is well-versed. Her father would permit her to sit in his court from a very young age. There, she learnt about politics, the art of diplomacy and conversation.

A palanquin stands proudly in the hallway. A wooden cage-like structure. Elaborately embroidered curtains hang from the carved lattice-work windows allowing the ladies to peer out, but no one to peer in. With two long wooden poles on either end these palanquins, with their occupants, would be hoisted up by four 'bearers' and carried on their shoulders.

She explained this was the very one she sat in when she had met her future husband, a man she hadn't clapped eyes on until her wedding day. It was part of her dowry, and she travelled like that for years and years in purdah, allowing no other man to see her, only a trusted group of women. But this lady had other ideas.

Laxmi Chandawat has the most enchanting of faces. Alert, attentive and full of life. She was a rebel, she learnt to drive a car. She giggled so much while she recounted how she would persuade her driver to take her into the deserted forests. There, she would pull back the heavy curtains and peer out of the front window. This was, of course, unheard of. Rajasthan was - and still is - an extremely conservative state, steeped in the caste system. At the age of 45, having had six children, she felt the time was right and took action. With great courage, she left the feudal system she had been born into and made a public life for herself in modern-day India. She became the first woman in Rajasthan to denounce purdah - and ended up in Parliament. There, she campaigned for the rest of her working life for women's rights.

When I suggested she had been very brave, she quickly dismissed this with a note of exasperation in her voice. Maybe that is the mark of a true hero. She was continually criticised, even vilified. She was changing the social order and powerful men did not want this.

Still, at her grand old age, she has retained that determination and strength and immense interest in other people and their lives. I ended up telling her all about my travels and my family. She wasn't the slightest bit worried, unlike the majority of people I had met, that here I was on my own, a lone mature lady flitting around India.

Sitting in the sunshine listening to her, I felt so privileged to have had the opportunity to meet her. I asked her what her secret was. How had she stayed so young at heart, and still so feisty. She turned to me and said:

"Meeting people like you".

I was incredibly touched. I had kept her talking for so long she probably breathed a great sigh of relief when I eventually got up to go.

With love,

Angie

The Fort was a new inspection, the hotel had yet to open. My visit came about when I had been inspecting a small hotel in Jaipur and the owner had talked about her son's new venture. It sounded perfect, but first I had to get there.

The new property was set in the wilds of Rajasthan and turned out to be a hairy, six-hour drive away. As I manoeuvred myself into the old bone shaker, I swiftly realised this was not the car I had seen the day before. That had been a nice comfortable car with seats and a bit of air conditioning. After a long and fruitless conversation, I discovered that the car I was supposed to have hired had to be used for another more important customer. I decided there wasn't enough time to negotiate, I would have to make the best of it. The back seat didn't exist and the front one was practically on the floor. The driver who I secretly wanted to scream at managed to terrify me at every opportunity.

Often, he would swig from a bottle of some highly suspect smelling liquid. As we travelled along he would wrench the door open and spit in the road. At one point, I believed he might fall out and I'd be left cruising along in the passenger seat.

We eventually arrived at the village after bumping along tiny side roads containing more holes than road. We swung in and out of the potholes at alarming speed. I hung on to the door with all my strength. I now have a sizeable indentation in the middle of my hand.

Bullock carts, camels, dogs and children greeted us. Mud huts, washing drying in the intense heat - hanging on walls, covering giant stones and most of the scrubby trees. Villagers washing themselves at the well while women stood patiently in line, collecting water, filling giant containers which were then placed on their heads. Vultures and buzzards patrolled the air like officious security guards, cruel, eager eyes gazing down at possible rich rewards. This was the India that few tourists had seen.

My bottom had now become devoid of any feeling, my back was screeching in pain. Clothes were stuck like glue to my hot and sweaty body. Not a good look for a first impression. As we juddered to a halt outside the most beautiful honey coloured palace, there was a long line of hotel staff waiting to greet me. Men dressed in glittering white outfits, their heads topped with deep red turbans spun with gold which matched the cummerbunds that encircled their middles.

I tried to smile and nod my head graciously all the while trying to forget about the sweat running down my legs. I was still swaying and unsteady from the violent rocking movement of the car and worried, in my present state, that there might be lots of stairs I would have to negotiate.

I noticed a young boy niftily wiping down my filthy, dust-covered suitcase. I then became aware of my feet. Looking down, they were the colour of dark clay. So many cracks in the car had let in half the desert. I could feel the hair on the back of my neck - sweat making nasty little clumps out of it. Any makeup I had applied that morning was probably halfway down my face by now.

The owner appeared, a handsome, assured man with an air of privilege that swirled around him. We were in the presence of his royal ancestors, generation after generation had lived here in this fort which stood dominating the village below. He greeted me warmly. If he was startled by my crazy appearance he didn't let on. We were to dine together tonight at 7pm.

I was given the royal suite, the Rani's room. Antique silver and wooden furniture, magnificent chandeliers which sparkled leaving droplets of light all over the walls. Window seats covered in such gorgeous fabric; it was impossible to sit on them. Tiny windows surrounded the rooms with lattice-worked marble. Everywhere there were intensely coloured stained-glass windows, their light dancing like magnificent jewels on each surface they touched.

This suite was for the Rani in purdah. Here she would live, only seeing her family and women servants, but by the careful execution of the tiny windows and the stained-glass she could observe the royal processions, the festivals and watch village activities without anyone outside of the palace ever seeing her. The literal meaning of purdah is 'a curtain, screen or veil'. It came from complex customs based on family honour, designed to maintain the sexual purity of women. Women had no voice, no free will, they only knew what their fathers, husbands and sons believed in. Women who showed any self-resilience or confidence were deemed in need of protection.

And here I was, occupying her private rooms. I would be sleeping in her magnificent bed, taking tea on her private terrace - a huge affair - with my own hanging seat covered in the finest deep red velvet while a soothing fountain could be heard tinkling nearby. Everything had been preserved and lovingly restored.

A bullock ride was suggested before darkness fell. Down the cobbled alley a group of children were waiting, excited and laughing. I might have been the first visitor they had ever seen. They were so sweet, desperately wanting to look at me, shy if I caught them staring. They would laugh and push each other in their embarrassment.

I watched as the old cart with enormous wheels was painstakingly decorated. Sumptuous fabrics the colour of jewels were carefully laid down. Garlands of flowers appeared, accompanied by bells and long brightly coloured ribbons. Silk cushions and velvet bolsters competed with each other, stacked high on a makeshift seat. The whole affair reminded me of a page in a childrens picture book. I was entering a fairy story and I was the main character. Even the two seemingly benign bullocks had their ears decorated, flowers sprouted from every part of their massive necks.

And so we started, with me sat in the back and the driver in front wearing a magnificent turban which I noticed, had been carried down from the fort with much ceremony.

The children were in raptures, running back and forth, weaving in and out of the tracks. Meanwhile I was sat amongst the finery with no idea where we were going. The sun had disappeared and now the oil lamps that danced backwards and forwards sent us swaying towards the village.

As we progressed, villagers started to appear and walk beside the cart. Babies in arms, pushbikes, dogs, motorbikes - all followed. Excitement mounted as the lights of the village slowly came into view. Outside every dwelling was the soft glow of oil lamps and braziers full of burning wood with huge pans set atop, ready for the evening meal. Two large heavy round stones were laid out, these would be used to grind the corn by the women, who would squat for hours at this task.

Now, villagers were coming from every home, hundreds of bodies seem to sweep us along. I felt like a complete fraud. We reached a crossroads and the cart stopped abruptly, every eye was on me. I had no idea what I should do but clearly something was expected of me. I tentatively stood up and said "Hello". The teacher in me must have kicked-in because for about ten minutes we had a very chaotic but entertaining English lesson.

Everyone took part from tiny children to the wizened, ancient ones, all repeating a few phrases I franticly thought of. I was surrounded by such goodwill and warmth.

Later that night I discovered that the villagers were keen for the fort to flourish. It provided much needed jobs and it was hoped that this would continue into the future - vital to the wellbeing of the local community. Most villagers eked out a living by farming the land, tough work, not enough work and not very profitable.

An exquisite table of startlingly white cloth - enormous - with starched napkins and crystal glasses was set on the terrace. The village was laid out before us. Wood smoke caught the slight breeze and wafted gently up. The rumbling of carts could be heard in the distance and the night with its warmth and jumble of enticing aromas enveloped us.

Dinner was delicious and exquisite, served by waiters whose waists were encircled by gold and silver cummerbunds, white gloves and scarlet buttons shining out of their pristine jackets. My dining companion was charming and informative and as I sat there, I thought of the Ranis in purdah. Did they ever have the joy of sitting here, right here on this terrace? Was it only the men who sat here while the women were locked in their sumptuous, beautiful prison?

Before bed, I stood on the terrace outside the royal bedroom. I looked through the stained glass which still seemed to hold the light. I looked through the miniature windows. I had to peer, I only got a tiny snapshot of the world outside. What a strange existence these women lived. I thought back to my time with Laxmi Chandawat, the first woman to come out of purdah in Rajasthan. I thought how brilliantly brave she was and just how much she had been able to achieve.

Breakfast this morning was a grand affair. Only me and the portraits of ancestors in the cavernous dining room. This was a land of heroes, a race of desert kings and Raiput warriors. The tales of valour and chivalry I had been reading about seemed to come alive. Women had burned themselves to death as their men rode to the final battle dressed in robes of saffron, the colour of death. They now looked down with their noble and terrifying faces as I ate my breakfast of cereal soaked in honey and cardamom, with cream delicately swirled on top, followed by hot buttery toast. My tea was poured from a huge silver teapot, my orange juice in a crystal glass. I savoured that moment as I knew I would soon have to get back into that excuse for a car and start the long arduous drive back.

With love,

Angie

Hello Everyone,

In a tiny village set in the Rajasthani countryside a guest house has been built. Amid the garden stands a temple, an ancient and sacred edifice. The owner of the guest house is a deeply spiritual man. His life is governed by his faith. He loves the world he lives in with a passion, believing he is meant to give back whatever he can. He does this by educating children on environmental matters. He's a wonderful human being and I felt so lucky to have met him.

He called me Angelina.

"Angelina you are truly fortunate to be staying here. For tonight, in this village, is the most important night of our festival. Tonight, if you would wish, you may witness the Night of the Answers". I jumped at the chance.

As dusk settled, I watched the courtyard fill. Women whose saris shone in the moonlight chanted and sang, often throwing themselves onto the floor with ethereal-like sounds emanating from their prostrated bodies. They banged their heads on the stone floors, which appeared to send them into a trance. The air was heavy and expectant with colour and passion.

The owner beckoned me to the entrance of the temple, a tiny structure of one room, built out of crumbling ancient stones. Here I watched as one Holy Man beat himself relentlessly with heavy chains, while another moved frenziedly up and down on the spot. The heat was almost unbearable from a fire that hissed and spat on a makeshift bench nearby. A heady mixture of incense, sweat, burning wood and mystery filled the room.

The priests now moved close to me and with much solemnity

asked me if I might have a question that I needed an answer to. Delicately, they gathered up corn and sandalwood, sifting through the pile to find the answer. Then, with a deep sense of gravity and grace, I was told the answer which immediately gave me much joy and reassurance (will let you know if it comes true). The owner of the B&B became very moved as the priests revealed that I must return one day so I could tell them if the prediction had come true. I then sat amongst the women who drew closer to me and I said my own prayers. I did feel that something truly significant had just occurred.

Throughout my stay the owner kept reminding me of this prediction and I made a promise to return one day.

Next morning as I sat having breakfast on the veranda, villagers started to arrive. They sat on the wall watching me as I munched on my toast, quietly studying me. The crowd then began to move - and I joined in. I had been told, a gentle warning perhaps, that an animal sacrifice was going to take place. Luckily, I had secreted some British Airways sick bags into my pocket, just in case. I desperately didn't want to embarrass the villagers, or the priests, or the lovely owner. I had been specially invited to the occasion, it was a great honour and I was told that no outsiders had witnessed this ceremony before. I was taken to the front, only yards from where the event was about to take place.

The Holy Men again seemed to be in a trance-like state. In the middle stood three young goats, strangely calm. An enormous scimitar was used for the deed. In quick succession I witnessed the executioner chop off each of the three goats' heads. Immediately the heads came off the blood was collected, warm and steaming, and given to the priests who quickly drank it. The bodies of the goats writhed around for a time afterwards. This was a bit distressing, watching those headless wriggling young bodies. It was a humane killing, probably far more so than what happens in many abattoirs around the world. The meat was to be distributed amongst the villagers for a huge feast that night. The whole village had been brought together for another year.

As I was leaving, I became aware that the Holy Men were taking a great interest in my camera. When I suggested that I might take a photo of them they jumped at the chance and then insisted I should be in it. They quickly rearranged their turbans, polished their medals and pulled up their trousers. I've a shot of me positioned in the middle of them. I'm twice as tall and three times as wide as them - and all of us are grinning madly.

With love,

Angie

Dear Ones,

I'm inspecting a delightful hotel with an equally delightful owner. He joins me for a drink after I've eaten the most delicious dahl and rice; flavours that mingle exquisitely, carefully cooked. I wonder how something so simple can taste so delicious. I try to behave myself but long to lick the plate before the waiter takes it away.

We sit on the roof terrace, the city twinkles before us spread out like a thousand jewels. The soporific air of India, heavy and warm, embraces us.

This owner is a liberal, informed, interesting man, in possession of a great sense of humour. I have done my research. He is a good man, aware of his responsibilities to his staff and to others. When I question him about his various charities, he dismisses them with a wave of his elegant hand.

"You know this country well, very well Angela, that is quite obvious". Our talk earlier had led me to tell him about my travels around India which had started more than thirty years ago.

"It is a land of extremes. I was born lucky, never to know hunger, to have many roofs over my head but others are not so fortunate. I have, they have not". And that was that, subject closed.

He had inherited this beautiful building. It was one of the many places he stayed in as a child in the school holidays. He has now turned it into a charming hotel.

He knows what his guests require. Every wall gleams - the whiteness of the paint shimmers in the intense heat. Crisp white linen adorns big comfy beds, not a speck of dust to be seen. Young men constantly sweep, wielding their brooms like dancers. They too, dazzle in their white uniforms and merge into the very fabric of the building.

It is nearing the end of one of many Hindu festivals. I've been hearing music and voices as the sun went down and longed to investigate but my complete lack of any sense of direction could prove problematic, those narrow streets all seemed to merge into one another.

"Angie," the owner softly said, "maybe you would care to watch some dancing tonight?"

I almost took his arm off.

We leave, accompanied by four hotel staff. They walk near me, deferential, gentle, pointing out the many potholes and gently directing me through the ever-increasing crowds. The air is heavy and thick and full of promise. I am wearing my new shalwar kameez and hope to blend in but, of course, I don't; with my short red hair and a head taller than almost everyone around me. We weave through the throngs of people and like magic, they part for us. We are pushed up some rickety old wooden stairs and emerge on a raised floodlit platform. Just the hotel owner and me, and the huge crowd below us.

I feel a bit like the Queen when she stands on the balcony of Buckingham Palace, but this is a wobbly, makeshift arrangement and besides, she hasn't got bright orange chrysanthemums sprouting from every corner of her balcony.

I'm invited to join in the dancing. I stand next to impossibly beautiful young girls, shining eyes and saris of flaming reds, greens, oranges, and yellows – and sway to the beat. I'm given a pair of sticks and shown how to dance with them. I try hard not to poke my partners' eyes out, or my own. I'm hopelessly uncoordinated and keep tripping into all around me. My sticks go flying up into the air, which makes everyone laugh. I seem to have a huge audience: street vendors, policemen, school children, fathers with children on their shoulders, mothers holding giggling babies - even a few cows who loiter in the midst of this marvellously chaotic and jolly scene with an air of bovine indifference. A sense of joy, elation and mischief-making pervades the night.

The dancing comes to an abrupt halt and again I'm bundled up to the makeshift platform. A man standing opposite on another makeshift platform, with an impossibly large microphone bellows into it. Now, all eyes are on the hotel owner sitting next to me.

He's a Rajput, part of the Udaipur Royal family. He's so self-effacing, he refuses to tell me what is being said about him. A huge orange garland is placed reverentially around his neck and the crowd bows low. He nonchalantly shrugs his shoulders when I suggest they must be saying what a very important person he is. He has a twinkle in his eye, he knows what's to come.

The chap with the huge microphone continues to regale the crowd and now I become aware the attention has shifted. Hundreds and hundreds of pairs of eyes are now focussed on me.

'Angela Reeeeeeeed' keeps being repeated and with every repetition the speaker becomes more animated, bordering on frantic. Another huge garland appears and is laid gently around my shoulders. The massive crowd of people bow low and I stand there wildly grinning, thinking I will never forget this time. I look towards the hotel owner and notice he is having a quiet chuckle. He turns to me, smiles, and says in a conspiratorial voice,

"It seems we have a very important person with us tonight".

With love,

Angie (a very important person)

Beautiful, romantic, gentle Udaipur.

I spend the afternoon visiting the City Palace. The tour guide is a delight and appears quite ecstatic when I ask question after question. I was so enthralled by everything I saw and stood resolutely right next to him, listening to his every word.

I unfortunately was placed with a group of American tourists. Weary, hot and bothered, their itinerary was brutal. One of the group tiredly explained,

"We're just palaced out".

The Palace is flamboyant, loud, blousy and completely gorgeous. It overlooks the lake and behind the exquisite façade there are other palaces, all eleven of them. Built out of granite and marble, it sparkles and shines in the sunshine. A fairy tale with so much romance.

There are oodles of balconies and towers intricately carved, fancy and fabulously ornate. Everywhere is delicate mirror work, marble carvings, and murals. Paintings vie with exquisite silver work, stunningly beautiful inlays on tables and chairs and cabinets that take your breath away. It's like walking into a mysterious dream and for a moment you are part of it.

I now became a bit hysterical, like a child let loose in a sweet shop. There was so much of it, it was so hard to decide where to look. I didn't want to miss a thing, but the exhausted and now impatient Americans had other ideas which they voiced loudly. They wanted to rush through, I wanted to linger. There was an awkward moment where I behaved like a bit of a diva. I could hear myself becoming posher and posher, I was almost turning into a Hyacinth Bouquet as I informed the rest of our group, that

I was going to see everything on offer, and would take my time. The lovely guide then became quite frenzied, he moved even closer to me and I fancied he was longing to hug me. He was so proud of his palace, he had such enthusiasm for his work and longed to convey it.

While the rest of the group were looking disgruntled, my guide with great delight took me aside. It was all a bit clock and daggerish as he motioned to a slight crack in a partitioned off wall. I screwed up my eyes and peered in. A huge, magnificent room without a soul in it. Little did I know what was to come, as I secretly spied the royal residence.

I am inspecting an enchanting country house. The owner's wife is one of the personal secretaries to the Maharaja. He and his wife and I talked until the early hours. As I leave the dining room, I am asked if I would like to join them at the Palace tomorrow, there I might have a chance to meet the Maharaja of Udaipur.

I go to bed, but excitement gets the better of me and I stay up half the night wondering what on earth I am going to wear, to maybe meet a Maharaja.

to: family and friends

from: Joyful Traveller

subject: The following day

The day before I was just an enthusiastic tourist, today I am being admitted to the royal palace as a guest. A magnificent man decked in rich red clothing, an exquisitely elaborate turban on his head, welcomes me with open arms and I'm there, on the guest list. We are admitted with much reverence and shown into the private quarters.

The room is utterly scrumptious, it's like walking into a box of jewelled sweeties. You remember those squidgy soft fruits? My mother used to love them, brightly coloured sugary treats. The room is like that. Everywhere you look something is glistening, shinning and dancing with the sunlight, that pours in through the gigantic windows whose velvet drapes have been flung aside.

Larger than life portraits of ancestors hang from every conceivable space, they look down through their exquisite sculptured noses on us mere mortals.

I'm introduced to the Princess, she laughs as she examines the salwar kameez I am wearing, the one I stayed up half the night deciding on. She tells me that a few days before she had bought the exact one and thought about wearing it today. She then sweetly tells me that I suit it more than she does, utter rubbish of course, but she is gracious and kind. We talk about our love of Fab India, a wonderful collection of shops dotted all over India selling beautiful but inexpensive clothes.

I find out she has a brother, the heir to this Indian dynasty. He will one day take over the running of the hotels which his father owns but for now he is a kitchen porter in Australia, learning from the ground up. I start liking this family very much.

This select little gathering turns out to be a press conference, a launch of a poetry book with all the profits going back into the

Maharajas charity. This Maharaja is a decent man. I know this from my conversations with local shop keepers, waiters, hotel staff, cafe owners, and tour guides, all seem to adore him. There are dozens of schools, colleges, women's workshops and health centres which carry the name of his charity.

And then he appeared this rather magnificent man. I watched intently as other guests are introduced to him. I'd heard that in India when meeting a very important person touching their feet is a sign of respect. I started to have a little panic. Now I decided I hadn't quite worked out what part of his foot I should touch. Would it be his ankle? or maybe his shin? might I offend him if I touched his big toe? Either way I decided I would attempt a curtsey. I did a bit of bobbing up and down and must have looked utterly ridiculous.

As he reached out to shake my hand, I got so flustered I blurted out that I had heard so many lovely things about him. He is a great bear of a man with a thick white beard and a fabulously handsome face. He turned slightly away from me and with a sideways smile and the biggest twinkle in his eyes said,

"I shouldn't believe everything you hear".

In that instance, I fell for him hook line and sinker.

We left through the Tripolia Gate, the gate reserved for royalty and important people. A small crowd were gathered and stared into the car. They waved so I waved back. I'm now practising my royal wave; you never know when I might need it again.....

So, I bid you all a goodnight and blessing my dears,

With love,

Angie

to: family and friends

from: Joyful Traveller

subject: Delhi, India - Shopping

Hello Lovelies,

I'm back in Delhi now. I met some Dutch tourists, all red-faced and cross. The bemused owner of the Internet café continued to grin, which made them even more bad tempered. It seemed that everything about India was hurting their sensibilities, the dirt, the noise, the chaos and the slow Internet. The whole crazy, colourful, extreme marvelousness of the place had completely passed them by.

There is an acceptance, a soul, a spirituality which seems to permeate the very fabric of this land. An ancient wisdom that dominates everything and everywhere. Kenneth understands this. These are the times when I miss him so much.

My day starts when I step out of bed and into my flip flops which I carefully position each night by the bed, even in the best establishments you're never quite sure what lurks on the floor. I know now that cockroaches make a crunching sound. I then begin to examine my body and count how many biting insects have managed to make a meal of me. I'm still nicely rounded so lots of tasty bits to choose from. This has become a morning ritual and something I do without thinking. How adaptable human beings really are. I am beginning to feel like part of the landscape.

Breakfast time is often a bit of a minefield. As I choose from the menu a little imaginary voice starts playing in my head and wonders if this bit of fruit or possibly that egg will have secreted away the dreaded E. coli bug, or worse. Every establishment I have stayed in thus far proudly announces in their brochure, 'DOCTOR ON CALL'. I have seen at least two tired, harassed docs with their large medical bags bulging with antibiotics and medicines to bung- up the tourist. When locals get sick they deal with it by eating rice, yogurt and bananas. Lots of tourists like to be close to a lavatory after they have eaten.

Breakfast and bowels over with, it's now time to brave the outside world. I step out into the street remembering to look down at the pavement, indescribable things are often down there waiting to be trodden on. I navigate my way around a large white cow munching away contentedly, totally oblivious to the demented traffic careering around it. I have now become so conditioned to my surroundings I don't give the creature a second thought. Spotted a monkey so quickly remove my sunglasses, an entertaining taxi driver told me that they only go for designer glasses nowadays, ha ha.

Manage to flag down a rickshaw. I know, off by heart, exactly what the exchange of words with the driver will be. I will ask him how much the fare will be to my destination and he will quote me some outrageous price, and smile. A bright red smile, his teeth stained red by the betel nut he chews all day. I then try and look aghast and quarter the price. We stand there and, as if by magic, other rickshaw drivers appear from nowhere. Indian rickshaw drivers seem to love a bit of drama. Maybe they are addicted to it as their whole life is one long drama on the road. And so, the scene takes on a bit of a merry get-together, everyone endearing and possessing a sense of humour which carries through the many exchanges. Often one of the questions will be,

"Which country will you be coming from madam?"

The price is finally settled and both of us are happy. I'm still paying a ludicrous price, we both know that. As I sit there, exposed to the elements in something that resembles a sewing machine on wheels, I'm hoping desperately that the driver forgets any English he might know, but he doesn't. As the cars, the bicycles, the lorries, the cows, the camels carrying unbearably heavy loads, the trucks and goats compete with each other, he carries on turning around, smiling his red smile, and shouts something incomprehensible. I pray for my life. I now know always to remember to sit on the left-hand side of the rickshaw. All rickshaw drivers seem to spit. They spit constantly. The spit is bright red and copious amounts of it fly around the city. They tend to spit out of the right-hand side of the rickshaw. If you're unlucky it might get you, depending on which way the wind is blowing that day.

Shopping is excruciatingly annoying, frustrating and utterly hilarious. Most shop keepers I've encountered are magnificent salesmen, charming and helpful, possessing a wonderful sense of humour, especially when you come to pay. If you don't barter somehow the transaction has lost its importance for the seller.

Yesterday, I wanted to buy a white scarf, I didn't want any other colour.

I enter a shop containing mountains of scarves piled high along the walls, every conceivable colour you could imagine. A smiling salesman and his young assistant jump up, there is an air of expectation, a customer.

"Good morning. Do you have any white scarves?"

"Oh yes Madam, certainly Madam, lots Madam".

I take a seat and start to relax a little: bad move.

"But this is a pink scarf".

"Yes Madam lovely colour you think?"

"Yes, a lovely colour but do you have a white scarf?

"Certainly Madam, could Madam tell me from where she is being from?"

"England, but this is a blue scarf".

"Lovely country, some family in the north, very nice, very nice place"

He can see that I am getting hot, so he jumps up and puts his rickety old fan on at full blast. This has the most devastating effect; all the scarves start dancing in the breeze with the assistant frantically trying to catch them. It's total mayhem as they swirl around the room. He switches the fan off and a semblance of peace returns but my clothes start to cling to me.

"So, Madam, finest cashmere, best quality, no better quality for you. English lady from England and now special morning price only for you".

"But it's purple and I would like a white one".

I start for the door. I've now spent over a quarter of a hour looking at scarves of every colour imaginable, and I'm boiling and bothered and no longer interested in any wretched scarf. As I leave the salesman follows me out gyrating on the spot and calling after me. I don't want to offend him, his is so charming and concerned, so I stand there feeling hotter and hotter and listen politely to him....

"Madam, Madam my brother, he has white scarves, great selection, white scarves for you, here Madam, here Madam take card, very good price for you, valued customer, very good price, yes, yes, Madam, brother's shop just around next corner, he is expecting you".

I take the card, no energy left, tell the rickshaw driver I'll pay him a ridiculous price if he will just take me back as quickly as possible to the hotel.

The thin card is still in my hot sticky hand. I glance at it and there in loud, blue glittery print is written...........

MR VIMAL MATCHESWALA

PRESERVER OF THE FINEST LAMB AND MUTTON

With love,

Angie

I should have smelled a rat. My editor asked me to make a 'slight' detour to Bangalore. The slight detour involved over a thousand miles of travel away from my original destination. Some strange story about having to undertake a blind inspection, when places are seriously wrong, and you go undercover.

I tried explaining what an astonishingly long detour it would be, but she was having none of it. I had never done one of these inspections, so I was keen to learn the ropes. She was rather vague about it all:

"Just get there, have a look around and report back on what you find".

It was a hurried phone call, she seemed distracted and preoccupied. I wanted to find out more, but there it was. Go to Bangalore and check out this place. She was adamant it had to be done, so off I tripped.

I went to the Potty Patti Hotel in Bangalore. Dear Potty Patti, a small hotel I will always remember.

The day before, in my haste running for my standby flight, I'd sprained my ankle on the airport steps. I'd had to be pushed around in a wheelchair at Delhi airport and then shunted back and forth at Bangalore.

Then, there was a slight altercation with the taxi driver on my arrival at the hotel. The fare we had agreed upon appeared to have doubled - and now the place was shrouded in darkness. The electricity had suddenly ceased to be, not unusual. Ancient lamps, perched precariously, were burning everywhere. They gave off this strange glow that didn't help much to see in the dark and, as often happens when I go travelling, everyone wants to get involved.

Upon my arrival at the front door, were a large group of boys employees at the hotel, waiting for me. There was a strange expectant air as I struggled up the front steps. They all followed me into my room including the disgruntled taxi driver, all watching me very closely.

My ankle was throbbing, the taxi driver was still trying to rip me off after a hair-raising journey and it was dismally dark. I was also starving hungry and that day, I had started to feel rather homesick. In a foul temper, whilst trying to wrestle some more rupees out of my suitcase, I shouted at the driver. It was pride more than anything, I was being ripped off and there was nothing I could do about it.

In the middle of this crowded chaotic scene a voice suddenly wafted down from a minstrel's gallery above the room.

"What took you so long?".

I hardly dared to look up. For a split second it whizzed through my mind that maybe I'd started hallucinating. I'd taken too many pain killers and they were muddling my brain. There was a huge gasp from all around. The boys were jumping up and down, poking each other in the ribs unable to contain their excitement. I hesitantly peered up through the gloom and there, sitting with The Times on his lap and a whisky and water in his hand, was The Scotsman - as though he belonged there.

The boys cheered, they had all been party to the surprise, loving the excitement and managing to keep it a secret. Everyone was so happy. I ended up giving the taxi driver a huge, undeserved tip and thanked the Lord that I had been born with a strong heart.

Of course, there was no blind hotel inspection. Kenneth had been in cahoots with my editor. She had to get me to Bangalore to meet up with him. Amazingly, she managed to do it without giving the game away. I'm looking back now to a few days before. I started to become a bit anxious when I realised that some of the inspections for my next destination were in out of the way places. Fine, but not if you are a bit of a neurotic with a fiery imagination. I mentioned this to my loving husband, who completely dismissed my fears and reminded me that I was the one who wanted to go on this venture. He must have been saying this as he clutched his airline ticket.

Now, on to Kerala. The first stop is a B&B. A bungalow which lies deep in some spooky woods - one of the reasons The Gallant Scotsman came out to be with me. So glad he did, he's a bit of a special one this Kenneth.

Until then,

With love,

Angie

Hello Everyone,

Kerala, South India, often referred to as God's Own Country and I'm here inspecting a rather unusual place.

As we entered the building, I became aware of a variety of boxes strategically placed near the reception desk, asking for donations. Guests were informed that all profits from the hotel went directly to two orphanages. I wasn't convinced and needed to find out for myself if it was true and if there were indeed any orphanages.

Getting information out of the owner to begin with was like pulling teeth. He was defensive and awkward, and I began to think it was all a scam. But, as I proceeded to question him, something became glaringly obvious; this was a good man, a shy man who believed in something I had yet to discover.

I asked if was possible to visit one of the orphanages and explained I had been a teacher and I was passionate about education. He immediately came to life and his awkward shyness seemed to forsake him.

"Madam, it would be a great pleasure for me to arrange a visit for you, a pleasure indeed".

And then he told me the story:

A Keralan-born Carmelite priest had had a great yearning to see more of the world. His Order sent him to Belgium. He worked in an assortment of schools and orphanages and there he had a vision. Returning to his homeland he vowed he would build a school. He did, two small schools were opened but money and finance were always endless problems.

This is where his faith stepped in, to support the unswerving belief in his dream. Here's what happened next. His nephew had taken holy orders but love came knocking at the door, so he left the church to marry. He, too, was a dreamer and decided his life's work was to continue his uncle's vision.

That nephew was, and is, the owner of this very hotel. The hotel supports two orphanages, housing and schooling over 900 children.

I was allowed to visit both schools. I watched the boys attending a lively religious service with lots of laughter and singing. I stood in the playground as shyly at first, they showed off their football skills. A quiet, disciplined lesson followed, heads bowed over textbooks, serious studying was taking place.

The girls' school was a quieter place, full of timid giggling and soft whispers. A sense of order and attainment permeated every corner. Spotless uniforms, long glossy dark hair tied back into perfect plaits sat in orderly rows. Their thirst for knowledge and appreciation of life sprang out from their textbooks.

Lost fathers; fishermen who drown in great numbers off the coast of Kerala – resulting in poverty-stricken, broken homes. But these children were amongst the happiest I had ever encountered.

The hotel is an Ayurvedic spa and the Scotsman and I were given a 'wellness package'.

Kenneth managed to endure all the pummelling and prodding, showing remarkable resilience as his skin flared up and took on the hue of a bright red post box. He continued to look happy even when he was bathed in buttermilk and cinnamon, emerging smelling like a danish pastry.

I loved every crazy treatment, especially the 'cooling cure to the brain'. It involved a large brown heap of something that looked distinctly like a cow pat although they swore it wasn't - but I'm not so sure. This dark concoction sat on my head while a banana leaf covered it, making a rather unusual hat.

A group of Russian guests arrived, their cottages only a few yards from ours. They swigged down bottles of vodka while their evil smelling cigarettes created dark little clouds above each of their heads. Asking the gentle Ayurveda doctor why they would possibly want to come to a health spa he confided,

"They are throwing their money into the sea. They take no notice of me, prescribing remedies for them is a great waste of time" shaking his head sadly, then added,

"But the children benefit, that is what matters mostly". I agreed.

We'd almost got used to the filthy cigarette smell and the clanking of bottles, but the argumentative voices grew louder and louder. In the early hours of the morning, I had had enough. Throwing my dressing gown around me, I decided to confront them. I stormed out while the Scotsman advised caution and some deep breathing.

I started off with as much grace as I could muster. I think it might be a British characteristic: that measured negotiating tone coupled with deep politeness, mingled with an apology.

"I'm terribly sorry to bother you. I was wondering if you could possibly not talk so loudly, we can't get to sleep. Thank you so very much".

I stood there in my flimsy dressing gown looking like a complete twit. The extraordinary thing was that not one of them took any notice of me. I didn't exist. I almost had to check myself to see if I was really standing there. I started to get a bit agitated and placed myself right in front of them, still they refused to look at me. The minutes ticked by, with the smoke now seriously affecting my airways. An unpleasant, greasy-haired man with a snarling mouth started mercilessly jabbing his fingers towards me. Fingers covered in heavy gold rings, diamonds glinting like crazy disco lights. He spat on the floor aiming at my big toe.

I returned to our room. Kenneth now worried that I might self-combust, all that might be left of me would be a heap of burning dust. I was furious, but I would get my revenge.

Early next morning my plotting from the night before swung into action.

I waited until Kenneth had gone for a treatment - he would have stopped me otherwise, him being a wise man, who likes to keep the peace.

This disagreeable lot were late risers, eventually emerging from their cottages with terrible hangovers and filthy tempers.

I've always longed to be a singer. Unfortunately for them I have a singing voice that upsets even me. I began to sing. My arias savagely tore into the early morning air. I was getting into my stride, I whooped with feigned joy outside each room. I started reciting Shakespeare, all that drama school training now being put to good use. I allowed my voice to ricochet off windows and along the patio. I even banged on their doors. If they'd answered, I'd decided I would ask them if they had any requests.

It's been noticeably quieter these last few nights.

On Sunday morning I strolled off to church. I'd stumbled over a dear little church half hidden among the dense vegetation. Once brilliant white, it's walls were now peeling, old stones mingling with the paint from long ago. Stained glass, badly patched up, still valiantly managing to throw rainbows of colour onto the ground.

The congregation was sitting on the steps watching for me. The hotel owner must have warned them. Women, resplendent in their Sunday-best saris, an odd assortment of men and the most wonderful ancient priest. He shook my hand and the warmth of his greeting travelled up through my spine. His teeth were few but his smile was contagious. I tried to explain that I wasn't a Catholic; this was going to be a Catholic mass and in the local dialect. He just grinned that grin and waved his hand saying,

"We are all God's creatures, come, come".

As happens so often in India, women look out for one another. The government tries to safeguard them, especially when travelling. Women-only ticket queues in train and bus stations, women-only train carriages. Now, these women gathered around me. Their kind-heartedness and gentleness touched my very soul and together we made our way into the church. I sat down amongst them on an ancient wooden pew, mottled and potholed with woodworm, worn thin by bodies over the years.

The service began and I was swept away by the faith and the grace laid out before me.

As the end of the service approached, the women knelt as the priest showered them with holy water. I tried to follow but didn't quite manage to kneel in time. The priest, much shorter than me, tried in vain to anoint me but almost floored me with the heavy, brass water shaker. Laughter shook the saris and, for a moment, I wondered if he had given me a black eye. He hadn't, it was close, but if he had, it would have been worth it.

When I came to say goodbye, the old priest took both my hands in his. He blessed me, then left me to make my way back along the tangled track to the hotel. As I walked, I felt such gratitude, humbled to be, for a short while, part of this place.

As I write this, I'm sitting at a desk with the windows open, the wind is raging outside. It's warm rain but gallons of it lashing down. The ocean is just yards from my desk, waves crash on the rocks.

Kerala is indeed God's Own Country.

With love,

Angie

to: family and friends

from: Joyful Traveller

subject: Mysore, India - Convicts and Noisy Cows

Hello Lovely Ones,

Wonderful scenic train ride from Bangalore to Mysore. All life is laid out before you on Indian railway embankments, a theatrical experience. Peering into dwellings often fashioned from bits of old cardboard, a few lone stones and lots of nasty black plastic. I watch women sweeping. Always sweeping that soft dust that invades the very soul of this land. See children bathing in old tin baths, eyes laughing watching the tourists stare out of the window. I wave and they eagerly wave back, a tender moment between us. And wish I was someone who could have the courage, the energy, the money, the faith to maybe open a little school here. Literacy rates in parts of rural India are still low, but I haven't, so I just smile.

A journey of approximately three hours, but this is never a reliable reckoning. A journalist writes in a tourist magazine,

"The most punctual train is the Yesvantpur Mysore Passenger service which reaches Mysore Junction with an average delay" but he doesn't go on to tell the reader what an average delay might be!

Decide this time to splash out and get posh seats; £9 each and that's with air-conditioning. The Second Seater passengers pay around 82p. The Scotsman says he remembers the last time we travelled economy class on a train in the Far East and then I remember too and how extraordinary it all was....

We were in Sri Lanka; I remember it as clear as day. We were on a long stopover together in the late '70's, spoilt B.A. cabin crew. We boarded a train in the 4th class carriage. Full to the very brim with bodies, and sat amongst a small herd of goats, chickens in wire cages, and some unseen creatures secreted away in baskets. Maybe they were snakes or mongooses? The baskets would lurch violently every now and again. I longed to find out what was in them. The owner looked rather guilty and would furtively cover the baskets with a dirty old cloth, frayed with holes, which I tried to peer through, unsuccessfully.

Everyone stared at everyone else and especially at me. Aren't human beings so fascinating. All of us are made of the same stuff, but we can look so remarkably different. There I am with my bright red, short hair and large feet. The ladies sit so easily, they allow their bodies to roll with the train. I'm stiff and awkward, worried I might tip over and flatten them. The women are thin and fragile looking but when I looked closer I could see their muscles, taut and powerful. Mine were poor things encased in a layer of fat.

These are working women. You see them on the sides of roads, on building sites, hacking at rocks then heaving baskets of them onto their heads, to carry long distances. It's always the women you see doing this heavy manual work.

Now, their saris, full of colour, were dancing in the wind which blew from the open window. The gold in their ears and their jangling collections of bangles glinted in the sunshine. I was in beige linen without a scrap of jewellery, feeling dull and unappealing.

The carriage doors were wrenched opened at a station which seemed to be in the middle of nowhere. I heard them before I saw them. Manacles around their ankles, handcuffs and chains which seem to wind around both prisoners made a terrible, strange, clanking noise. They manoeuvred themselves into seats opposite us. A prison guard between them resplendent in his dark green uniform with a strange jaunty hat poised atop his black, slicked-back hair. Either side of him were the pathetically thin and miserable convicts. Dressed in uniforms so faded the pattern of the cloth was hard to make out. Ancient clothing covering their bony bodies. We sat for a while; I didn't like to look at them. I was feeling embarrassed and fascinated but didn't want to upset them. Equally, I was feeling so sad wondering what awful crime they might have committed. Their feet were tightly bound in iron with just a small amount of chain between each leg that allowed them to walk, impossible to run trussed up like that. I was peering at their feet and traced the heavy chains up to their hands. Bulky iron handcuffs circled each wrist. The weight must have been damaging, their hands sunk into their laps.

When I'm nervous I fiddle with my earrings. This time I was fiddling an awful lot more than usual and one small gold earring fell out of my right earlobe. I felt self-conscious and incredibly uncomfortable and pretended not to notice. I had spied it roll under one of the convicts, and they had noticed. What happened next was something I will always remember. They struggled to stand up. Then, with a tremendous amount of effort, knelt on the floor of the train anxiously trying to find my missing earring. The prison guard was now very animated barking orders at his charges. The prisoners started to chat to him and to each other. Success! The prisoner on the left had found it. He ceremoniously handed it over to the guard who, with a flourish, held it high and then laid it reverently into my open palm.

The other passengers throughout this little interlude seemed to be as memorised as I was. When it was found they jumped up with lots of vigorous clapping. The prisoners sat down with the officer in the middle and all three of them looked victorious. They beamed at me continuously. I noticed one of them, still a young man, had just a few broken teeth in his mouth. The guard puffed himself up and had a look of pride on his face as he sat between these two men he was taking to be incarcerated.

Back to Mysore. If an Indian city could be described as 'laid back' maybe Mysore could be that city; even the cows are quite content to be milked in the streets as the speeding cars and crazy tuk-tuk drivers whiz past. The cows are confident, calm and seem to be the ones who are in control. An explosion of fragrances and spices hit you between your eyes and little polite signs, my favourite 'Don't pluck the flowers', found in a park, with no flowers.

Life is played out on the streets. Barbers wielding terrifying cutthroat razors in tiny shacks, makeshift mirrors often broken hanging precariously from a rusty nail on a bit of wall.

Mysore is famous for its magnificent palace, which is illuminated each Sunday for an hour. A bit too Disney for me. 96,000 light bulbs burn for an hour at sunset and huge crowds gather in admiration, to stand and stare.

We were staying in an odd little establishment for the first two days. Incredibly cheap, the hole-in-the-ground lavatory gave it away, but the bed was quite comfy and the sheets didn't look like many guests had been sleeping in them. The area was noisy and squalid.

I kept sighting fabulous looking transvestites. Taller, some so breathtakingly beautiful it was hard not to stare. Men approached us and offered us everything humanly possible; drugs of every type, men, women, boys, girls - all tragically available. One nasty looking man joked he could get a good price for me.

We moved on to a decent, small hotel with a rather grandiose name, The Park Lane Hotel in a pleasant tree-lined street. The first night was spent in restless sleep due to the noise of India's scared animal, the cow. Hefty groups of them would congregate in the dead of night around the hotel's heavy, metal rubbish

sacred

bins parked in the street directly under our bedroom window. They were a ruthless demolition team. I got the impression that this had been happening for years. They had perfected their skills and over the bins would go, spilling their offerings. A little dinner party then took place with much mooing and chomping, interspersed with bad-tempered noises if one of them was being too greedy.

The next day, feeling tired, grumpy and sleep deprived I found the manager. Explaining the problem, I suggested they might move the bins to another area, possibly to the back of the hotel so guests would not be disturbed. He seemed mystified but, as is often customary here, was charming and accommodating.

"Madam, we will definitely see what can be accomplished".

That night, a violent argument broke out below our bedroom window. A posse of very bad-tempered cows, so indignant that their source of food had been moved, were now forming a protest group. They were loud and extremely outspoken.

I had thought to ask the manager why they don't just leave out the food for the cows - by-passing the bins – but this seemed too logical. So, when he asked me with a concerned brow the next morning,

"And how were you sleeping, Madam?"

I just smiled and told him maybe it would be better to move the bins back. He didn't enquire why that might be. He gently nodded his head from side to side and went on his way.

With love,

Angie

to: family and friends

from: Joyful Traveller

subject: Mysore, India - A wonderful tuk-tuk driver and the best masala dosa ever

Bibek was waiting for us outside our hotel, along with many other expectant tuk-tuk drivers. He stood there with his round sunny face almost willing us to step inside his vehicle. It's so uncomfortable, I stand there wishing I could ask all of them to ferry us around. I know how steeped in poverty they are, but Kenneth headed towards Bibek. This led to three cheerful days with him, even if we wanted to walk, we took his tuk-tuk.

He was fearless on the road and drove like a maniac, as do all tuk-tuk drivers. These miraculous vehicles remind me of sewing machines - sewing machines on wheels. Each one customised with various ribbons, banners, flags and assorted hanging paraphernalia. Enterprising drivers have even supplied a few cushions but Bibek's tuk-tuk was of the standard variety. With its iron bench seat which mercilessly slides you from one side to the other as you hurtle around corners, trying hopelessly to hold on to anything that looks vaguely stable.

Nothing was too much trouble for Bibek. He would happily take us up steep mountain sides, down tiny unmade roads, looking for the places tourists would not be found. He would inform us each day, that he would be outside our hotel early every morning. Even when we arranged a late morning time to meet, promising we would be there, he would have been patiently waiting for hours, certain of picking us up.

"MYSORE MASALA DOSAS, BEST IN THE WORLD", written on a billboard in bright red paint. It's true and we found the best ones in Mysore and all because of Bibek.

The masala dosa is an institution. With it comes great rivalry amongst cooks, believing their secret recipe is the best, and none more so than in Mysore. The people of this city consider the Mysore dosas to be unsurpassed. They stand apart from any others according to an article I read, dedicated to the extraordinariness of this particular dish.

"Madam and Sir, I'm taking you to a place - no tourists."

Bibek had got the measure of us right from the very beginning.

"No tourists, just local locals, very clean, very clean, best masala dosas in Mysore, no, no, I have to say, best masala dosas in the world".

And with that we were off. His excitement super-charged his driving, it became even wilder. Racing towards the restaurant, seriously wondering if we would get there in one piece -alive, or would we ever get to sample these legendary delights.

We tumbled out of Bibek's contraption, in front of a building that had stood the test of time and was still vaguely upright. Paint had peeled off the walls a long time ago. A spaghetti junction of electrical wires and cables hung down in mind-boggling bundles. We were in a run-down, industrial area and, yes, not a tourist in sight.

Groups of people were standing around or were crammed like sardines onto the plastic-covered benches either side of Formica tables. A place was found for us and we became the main attraction that morning, at least our appetites did. Hot chia was placed before us then the famous masala dosas arrived.

A masala dosa is a thin, potato-filled pancake accompanied with a sambar sauce and coconut and onion chutneys. The pancake is made from a fermented rice and black lentil batter; light and crispy, with a rich brown outside and a soft middle. I can honestly say, at that moment, biting into this creation was one of the most delicious culinary experiences I have ever had.

The gathered company watched with interest as we ate. The dosas kept coming and coming and we kept eating and eating. Bibek forgot to mention that unless you tell the cook you don't want any more, they just keep bringing them. I have no idea how many we managed to cram down our throats, but as we waddled out, we got a round of applause and the cook emerged from his cubby-hole to shake our hands.

While we were roaring around the city in his tuk-tuk, Bibek, with much pride and joy spoke of his daughter and her imminent marriage. He extended an invitation to us. I asked him how many guests he was expecting. Without batting an eyelid he said, "Around 700 Madam, and for two days" and then laughed so loud as he told us how, every day, he thanks God that he was blessed with only one daughter.

The cost of the wedding will almost destroy him. This is a man who earns about £2 a day. He repeatedly told us how it would have been a great honour if we could have been present. Sadly, we would have left Mysore by then or we would eagerly have gone. We gave him a big, fat tip hoping it would make a small contribution to the wedding costs of his only daughter.

This gentleman had enriched and brightened our time in Mysore. I only hope the wedding was a great success and made the father of the bride, a happy man.

With love,

Angie

Dearests Ones,

We left Kenya yesterday, and now sitting with my computer in a tiny hut on a gleaming white Zanzibar beach with a very unreliable Internet connection. It's fiercely hot but the cooling breeze from the sea, only a few yards away, wafts over me. I have to be quick as the electricity, too, has a mind of its own and continually cuts out, often as I am just about to press SEND.

Kenya was so beautiful although the little bits we saw of it were also complicated. Staying with old friends for a while gave us a glimpse into the world of expats, but this couple are not your typical expats by any stretch of the imagination.

Henry was born in Kenya, the son of veterinary surgeons, who were fearless, arrogant and intrepid. At the tender age of six Henry was packed off to boarding school. A hundred little boys cooped-up in the middle of the African savannah. As a rebel, he would sneak off with three of his friends to roam the land, making dens out of abandoned aardvark's hidey holes. At thirteen, when he wasn't being shunted back and forth to his hated British boarding school, he was free to roam the plains. Unbelievably, he was allowed to take-off on a horse for days at a time with a friend, a .22 rifle to shoot Guinea fowl and small antelope in the dry season; and a sleeping bag which he slept in under the African stars. I think this is where he learnt to be fearless and part of the landscape. Henry has a wild, irresistible charm. He belongs here, the huge skies do not dwarf him, the wildness and beauty are in his soul, I don't think they will ever leave him.

Sally is also a fearless soul, they go together very well. Brave, imaginative, compassionate, loving and possessing a ferocious social conscience coupled with a wicked sense of humour, she fits in here marvellously.

Before our arrival, while driving through the streets we notice every house is surrounded by high walls with barbed wire cascading everywhere like flowing rivers. Large notices abound warning of CCTV cameras in operation 24/7. It was all quite unsettling and I started to feel rather intimidated. Leaving home, we naively hadn't given our safety a second thought. We knew Henry and Sally were well acquainted with this part of Kenya but, they weren't your typical ex-pats.

We arrived in the dead of night. The taxi driver turned his engine off and pointed to a dark lane flanked by high walls on either side.

We peered into the darkness and spied a gate and beyond that a wooden hut. Wedged into the entrance was a very old man with a bow and arrow - fast asleep. I gently touched his arm, no movement. Kenneth did quite a bit of clearing of his throat and with a gentle stirring the old chap opened his eyes. His face became engulfed in an enormous smile, the couple of his remaining teeth joining in. He seemed delighted to see us and motioned us towards the house where Sally and Henry, in their pyjamas, were coming up the path.

After we apologised for waking the old man, I had a fit of hysterical laughing as Sally explained that this was their night watchman. We got into bed and decided we had two choices: (a) make some awful excuse and leave - maybe even tell them the truth that we just couldn't cope with the lack of security or (b) we could trust that nothing was going to harm us. We choose the latter, vowing to each other that we would shelve our fears and enjoy every moment.

Sally and Henry have become part of the community though some of the other expats find them irritating and unsettling. Unfailingly generous with the people they employ; they have helped their cook build his own house and they paid for their gardener to go back to school. On a visit to her parents, their daughter, a doctor, diagnosed the ancient night watchman as being severely anaemic, he's fine now.

People would constantly appear on the doorstep. It seemed like Sally and Henry had set up their own little bank. People either paying money back or asking for more. Sally and Henry were supporting numerous small businesses, and local people were encouraged to set up ventures on their own such as one chap who started his own tuk-tuk taxi business. In a shed in the garden there was an innovative project run by local people where old green glass wine bottles and Coca Cola bottles were sawn in half, smoothed down and fashioned into drinking glasses.

The beautiful house, open to the elements and built on a craggy cliff set above the Indian Ocean, contains their treasured possessions shipped all the way from Somerset. But, it's not an easy life. Violent, armed robberies are not uncommon. Most properties belonging to the expat community, or the emerging Kenyan middle-class, are surrounded by brutal barbed wire fencing, heavy iron gates and security cameras at every turn. Not Sally and Henry's house.

"One day we might be robbed", says Henry in a matter-of-fact tone. This is the price they are both prepared to pay to live here, where Henry grew up and where is heart is. They are not prepared live in a prison, or in a state of constant fear.

They both volunteer for a local charity which supports the poorest of the poor, placing children into schools. I went out with Sally and one of the placement staff and watched her interview a mother. We drove down unmade tracks for miles finally arriving at a tiny hut made entirely of mud. Just inside the door was a place for the one goat they owned, and then two broken beds stood on a mud floor which floods when the rains come. Seven of them live there - with nothing. We took them an odd collection of second-hand clothes. One tiny child took a man's vest and she shyly paraded around the hut dragging the vest through the mud, feeling like a princess.

Access to clean running water is still a huge problem. Women, with huge plastic bottles on their heads, carry water weighing as much as 3 stone often two or three times a day and sometimes walking many miles. It's a myth to say it makes them strong, what it does is ruin their necks and many women suffer a lifetime of constant pain.

We drove down a brand-new road which was beginning to show signs of wear. The tarmac should have been laid to a certain depth but the money to finance the road had been siphoned off in bribes and backhanders. It ended up as a wafer-thin road surface with potholes already in evidence.

The people we met were so warm, friendly, generous, enthusiastic, obsessively polite and with a genuine love for their country.

There were times when I felt scared and anxious; then it became a bit like a Famous Five adventure. We'd go off for a trip up the creek in a small boat and its engine would often cut out. One trip, in the middle of a game reserve in Sally and Henry's rather dodgy car, we found ourselves surrounded by a herd of elephants. But looking back now, it was the pirates that still give me goose bumps. There's Sally and I having a natter on the beach, a bit of a sunbathe and then a lovely swim. I'm staring out to the horizon watching two ships not that far away. Old rusty hulks looking like something out of an adventure book. I causally turn to Sally and enquire what sort of ships they could be. "Oh those, they are Somali pirates".

I'll write with news about Zanzibar, not quite sure what to make of it yet, but will let you know.

With love,

Angie

I have tried for days, very unsuccessfully until now, to write to you. This computer has become so hot that it will probably combust before I finish - possibly taking me with it.

The long rains are expected soon; rains that last for months and almost drown the island. Everything is winding down. The hotels are weary; the waiters return to their villages to plant crops. Huge black crows cry incessantly, an unfortunate legacy from the days of British rule.

The Indian crow was introduced by a short-sighted, rather stupid British Governor. They are a terrible menace now. Their original job was to get rid of the hordes of rats that infested the island back in the 1800s. All that's happened is that these horrid bullies have decimated many indigenous bird species - and the rats are still happily living here. The crows stare down at me while I lie by the pool, horrid little yellow eyes watching; they gossip and bicker with each other.

Zanzibar is so beautiful yet so troubled. It is paradise, dazzling white beaches and swimming in a sea the colour of sapphires. We eat delicious fish, we watch the boats land with their catch almost in front of us, drink divine cocktails every evening as the sun goes down. It's when you start asking questions and travel through the countryside you sense a different story.

We are now in the South of Zanzibar having started off in the North, we've tried to make sure that everywhere we stay supports the local community in some way. In the past few years, hideous great all-inclusive resorts have sprung up around the island with thousands of foreign tourists who eat, drink and bake themselves into a stupor. According to the many local people we've met, the money which the resort developers were obliged to give to the government to support local infrastructure projects in surrounding villages - just disappeared. This has resulted in unmade roads, no hospitals and expensive schooling and medical care. Poverty and living conditions outside the resorts are poor. This is irresponsible tourism at its worst. Why have we been so blind to this?

The Maasai are nomadic warriors and herdsmen; they've done that for ever. Tall, fierce, upright, they don't walk so much as glide, their spines ramrod straight. I watch them intently longing to emulate their graceful poise and movement, me clumsy and heavy limbed. Impossible. I longed to have a conversation and when Kenneth and I were walking along the beach I tried to maneuver my way into the hideous looking all-inclusive resort. There were three Maasai gentlemen who were guarding the entrance. They wouldn't let me in, I didn't really want to go in, I wanted to find out more why they were here, a long way from home. They suffered all my questioning with humour and bemused politeness.

It seems that during the tourist season the Maasai come to Zanzibar from their homelands on the borders of Kenya and Tanzania to work as security guards/night watchmen for all the big hotels. They are more or less forced to come here because both governments have decided that money-making is more important than people. Tourists paying huge sums of money for wild-life safaris are far more lucrative than having the indigenous nomads, the rightful inhabitants on the land. Much of the land where the Maasai roamed free for generations has now been turned into profitable game reserves where local people see little, if any, of the vast amounts of money that disappear into government "black holes". Some of these proud and noble Maasai men are now reduced to being night watchmen.

Still carrying their ceremonial swords, and large clubs, they are a formidable presence. Some stand, resembling flamingos, leaning on their sticks for hours and hours, completely still, and some of them are not only night watchmen: women from Northern Europe often come here hoping to get to know them better.

I became intrigued as I watched rather sad, middle-aged women, a hint of desperation in their eyes, at breakfast with their warriors.

One morning I was approached. This beautiful man offered me his personal services. Choking over my poached eggs I thanked him and told him I was waiting for my husband. He grinned telling me I didn't know what I was missing, sauntered off leaving me wondering, as he turned the corner and waved at me.

Stone Town is part of the old trade centre of the capital, Zanzibar City, and it was here that the world's last open slave market existed. Over 70,000 slaves were sold in the market place each year. Missionaries are often criticised but it was here that Dr. David Livingston and the Bishop of Zanzibar helped to end the slave trade; they are credited with smuggling many slaves away to freedom.

Before we were allowed the see the place where slaves were held, our guide insisted we visit the interior of the Cathedral. It was just Kenneth and I in the tour party. We were shown the exact spot where the whipping post stood – and I broke down in tears. The high alter now covers the post and is surrounded by a white stone circle encased by a red one. The red stones symbolize the blood that was shed and, in that moment, somehow the whole horror of this place came alive. The guide gently led me out, his hand resting on my back as Kenneth followed.

We stood in the courtyard where the slaves would be lined up; the tallest at one end, the smallest at the other. To test the strength of these souls they were routinely whipped with a stinging branch. The ones that did not cry out, faint or show their pain would fetch a higher price.

The dungeons were long, dank and dark. A stone shelf ran the length of this low stone building where bodies were packed like sardines in a can. Underneath this shelf on the stone floor yet more bodies would be crammed together. Those were the ones who had survived the journey; a third of slaves died at sea. Rusted chains and manacles lay like instruments of torture.

Places are said to store memories. I stood there and started to choke; my skin grew clammy. I began to shake and the souls of all those dead men, women and children seemed to rise up before me. The guide could see my panic and again, carefully and with much kindness, led us out.

Stone Town would make the perfect location for an action movie, it probably has. Its dark, atmospheric, narrow, winding, cobbled alleyways are full of street vendors, bikes, carts, donkeys, motorbikes, food stalls, spice markets and an impossible jumble of electrical cables that tumble down from the decaying stone buildings. It's a mysterious, intoxicating, heady mixture of Arab, Indian and African cultures.

Soaring wooden doors are elaborately carved with imposing brass studs which, in a different era, the residents hoped would deter rampaging elephants.

Off to Dar es Salaam tomorrow on a creaky old ferry. Should be interesting. I'm determined to keep my suitcase with me; Might be a problem; can just see me in the hold hanging onto it.

With love,

Angie

Dearest All,

Getting on the Zanzibar-Dar es Salaam ferry was indescribable mayhem. Hordes of porters, taxi drivers, hawkers, and some dubious looking characters surrounded the passengers. It was so very hot. Sweat ran down most faces. The unremitting noise seemed to reverberate, getting louder and louder as everyone waited for the ferry to appear.

I wanted to be in with the action, so Kenneth and I stayed behind in the shade with the local travellers. Fortunately for us, we were sitting beside a lovely young chap who was more than happy to interpret what happened next.

An official looking character got up and started a long, impassioned monologue; he could have been delivering a Shakespeare speech, one of the tragedies. Lots of locals were muttering and looking very fed-up.

Apparently, they are trying to stop local people from rushing onto the ferry as there have been several fatal accidents. The mutterings were about the 'muzungos', the tourists and why they were able to wait at the front of the queue. One of the passengers pointed out that the muzungos' tickets are more expensive. Then one bright spark in the audience - which had now taken on quite a jovial air - winked at me saying it was a stupid idea, as white people have skin that burns in the sun and they should be back in the shade letting the locals on first.

He was completely right. Glancing over and watching the tourists with so called 'posh' seats sweltering and turning redder in the heat as they waited at the front of the queue.

Then it happened; someone spotted the ferry and all hell let loose.

We were propelled along by the crowd with me furiously clutching my precious suitcase that I was determined to keep with me. This was bodily wrenched out of my hands and disappeared. The vessel appeared, the colour of nutmeg which, on closer inspection was, actually rust that had engulfed most of it. Occasional clusters of paint peered through. Above the ear-splitting din, you could hear the groan and grinding of rusted metal on rusted metal.

Two and a half hours later I sent a silent prayer of thanks towards the horizon as we spied dry land. Everyone elbowed each other out of the way, and I lost Kenneth yet again. Teams and teams of porters and taxi drivers descended on the mob of passengers, and then one beaming man spotted me. He must have seen the desperation in my eyes (all those lovely summer frocks, never to be seen again). He lunged for my hand and held it tightly, pushed me into the crowd, wheedling his way to the front while continuing to clench my hand. We stood there on the jetty and must have made a very strange sight; holding hands and standing very close to one other - he came up to my waist. As our suitcases were tipped out of the boat, he caught them magnificently. He was so thrilled that the right suitcase had been delivered to the right recipients he gave a little jig on the spot.

Meanwhile, Kenneth had met a taxi driver who assured him he knew 'exactly' where our guest house was located. Just before the taxi door closed his cousin smartly nipped in and sat beaming in the front. He'd decided to come along for the ride.

The guest house was supposed to be no more than twenty minutes away. Two hours later we were still driving around the city. The taxi driver and his cousin appeared to have had a great time. Lots of chats, we all put the world to rights, talked about our life back home, heard about their large extended families; they didn't want the journey to end.

Eventually, they managed to find the guest house and we arrived there in darkness. Lamps with no bulbs; doors which didn't lock so you'd have to jam them shut with a chair; mosquito nets with holes flapping about; a fan that made so much noise that if you kept it on there would be a strong possibility of going deaf overnight - and various odd insects and creepy-crawlies in the shower and lurking under the bed. The husband-and-wife team who ran this place were so kind, so accommodating and so cheery ..... that it was all Okay.

We spent the rest of that night at the bar swapping stories with locals and other visitors. They slapped their thighs and nearly fell off their bar stools when I regaled them with tales of our ferry ride and the porter whose imprint was still on my hand.

Finally, we retreated to our bedroom. It didn't matter that nothing seemed to work. The electricity had now disappeared, the wildlife was still under the bed and the curtains refused to close. We slept and I dreamt of our standby flight the next day with a bit of me hoping we wouldn't get on – so wouldn't have to leave.

With love,

Angie

Dearests,

What sort of person would go on a walking pilgrimage, covering over 120 kilometres often having to scramble up steep hillsides, then down quite torturous stone-laden paths, without doing any training beforehand?

Obviously one of little brain, or maybe possessing an arrogance of huge proportions. I've been in a bit of discomfort since we started, but the beauty of the place and the joy of walking alongside Nessie, makes the pain magically disappear.

Today though, my legs feel like leaden weights. They ache horribly but my dreams are of reaching the famous square in Santiago de Compostela with my Pilgrim passport which, hopefully, will hold the precious stamps. At each official stop you are given a stamp. At the end of this journey the passport is checked and, if in order, you are then declared a "peregrina"; a real pilgrim.

Teams of stout, disciplined Germans start off at the crack of dawn. We tend to miss them by many hours, but then incur the heat of the day. Somehow, it's a worthy trade-off for a leisurely breakfast of pastries and coffee. It makes it seem more like a jolly holiday rather than a serious task.

Sometimes we come across walkers who look desperately ill. You feel it might be the last walk they'll ever do. The Camino attracts a wide range of souls, all with their own stories: divorce, financial ruin, death of a loved one, religious commitments and many others just wanting to walk.

I wanted to walk with Nessie the ancient paths that thousands have done before. We wanted to go walking with a purpose, seeking something bigger than ourselves.

We tramp through tranquil fields, farmlands, vineyards, narrow streets and tiny paths. Forests of eucalyptus and pine trees overpower us with their energising smell. As we walk under their canopies we breathe deeply and our lungs expand. Scattered along the way are peaceful hamlets with a handful of homes and always a tiny church. Sometimes we come across an ancient structure that materialises in the middle of nowhere and there, nestling on the minute altar, is a lit candle and a bunch of flowers. These are precious moments, unexpected, treasured, where we rest and feel the gratefulness of just being alive.

We know which way to go. There are many signs. The scallop shell is what all pilgrims look for on gates, trees, railings, rocks, and buildings; all pointing the traveller in the right direction. No one is quite sure of the history of this symbol. Some say it was a practical item; a scallop shell which could be used to collect fresh water from the many streams and springs along the way.

We have a camera and take silly, rude faces of each other. Nessie tries to capture one of my many lavatory stops, which resulted in wet knickers and me yelling at her, once frightening a herd of goats, that rushed off in great despair. There is no Wi-Fi on this route and we have no mobile phones. There is only nature, our feet traipsing in the footsteps of thousands and thousands of pilgrims.

The Camino de Santiago or, The Way of Saint James, was originally travelled by King Alphonso the Second in the 9th Century. He wanted to confirm that the remains of the Apostle James, really were those. He decided they were and thus began the great pilgrimage.

Food keeps us going and as we walk, we have the identical conversation every day.

"I wonder what's for supper tonight", one of us will ask.

And then we describe our favourite Spanish dishes.

Cod is the national food treasure and dishes come in all shapes and sizes. Great platefuls of rich tomato stews laced with herbs and plentiful quantities of garlic, nestling amongst large chunks of gleaming white cod; fish cakes stuffed with minced cod and parsley, goujons of cod, the batter as light as a feather. Sardines are revered; grilled to perfection, served with huge wedges of lemon.

We stay in small guest houses whose owners and their ancestors have been running them for generations. These owners often ask about our day's walking, but this is just a ruse to get our attention. After they politely listen to our day's adventure, they start to talk. Their love of food is renowned. They give us lengthy descriptions of what is being served that night. It is a very personal affair and extremely important to them.

I warned Nessie that we had to listen - and look interested at whatever was offered, recalling the time Kenneth and I had mortally offended a chef in a small guest house in the north some years ago.

"Have you ever tried our famous percebes?", enquired the enthusiastic chef, smiling as if he was offering us a prized dish which not many tourists have access to. He then added,

"It's not on the menu but it's a, what do you say, a treat?"

He brought out the oddest-looking things, like squidgy-looking rocks with hidden eyes. With devotional-like intent, he held the small foot between his thumb and finger and pulled out a long piece of marbled matter, plonking it straight into his mouth.

Percebes, goose-necked barnacles, are a particular delicacy here. They attach themselves to sea-facing rocks. A dangerous and perilous job to wrench them off these places, hence their exorbitant price. They are revolting; a flavour so nasty I have no words to describe them. Only to say, it would be like swallowing a salty, fishy-smelling piece of rubber hose.

He watched as we valiantly tried to eat more than one. Anymore and I knew I would throw up. I tried explaining how interesting these delicacies were but maybe we shouldn't spoil our appetite for the main course? He flounced off and refused to have anything to do with us for the rest of the evening. We had committed a grievous crime.

If you are ever offered percebes, run a mile. But you must try the pasteis de nata. A mouth-watering crunchy, flaky pastry loaded with the smoothest, creamiest custard concoction ever invented.

As some of you know, my hair colour while living in Spain has caused me great concern. I approach these awful hair salons where everyone seems to be wearing a 'mullet' and mistakenly believe them to be capable of giving me a vibrant, exciting hair colour. Invariably, I end up looking like a large carrot.

So, there is Ness and I walking the Camino through woods and fields, walking our way around Spain. Ness with her curls flying, adorned with colourful hair accessories and jewellery and an assorted mixture of clothes bought from around the world. I still doggedly have my pearls around my neck, they seem to go nicely with my ripe, tangerine-coloured hair. We make an odd couple - nothing like the other peregrinas.

Nessie is the most sunny, forgiving and inspiring walking companion anyone could ever have.

Another twenty kilometres and we'll be there. Think of us, even if it's only to have a laugh at my hair colour and numerous blisters.

"He who would valiant be
'gainst all disaster,
......to be a pilgrim."

With love,

Angie

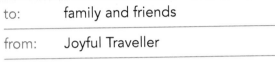

to: family and friends

from: Joyful Traveller

subject: Bogor, Java, Indonesia. 2012 -
Falling into a paddy field

Nessie has become part of the community here and knows almost everyone we pass in these tumble-down, ram-shackle streets. She seems to know every street twist and turn and as we navigate them, people smile. Not a wan little smile but smiles that light up entire faces, they giggle with abandon. The most charming, delightful and gracious people you could ever hope to meet - and they all love Nessie.

Yesterday, the taxi we'd booked never appeared. While waiting in the street, a complete stranger insisted on giving us a lift. A twenty-minute journey and he wouldn't take a penny. We talked about life and our children and I mentioned how appalling the traffic was in Bogor. He seemed a bit perplexed, this was all he had ever known, far worse in Jakarta he'd been told.

Last night at dinner I sat next to Miguel, from South America. He is one of seventeen children from a village deep in the Amazon jungle. He left home at thirteen and tramped for four days to the nearest city. There, through a combination of luck and sheer tenacity (years spent sorting rubbish and washing dishes) he ended up at Yale University in the USA and he is now a passionate environmentalist.

Opposite him sat Christine his wife, an American, fluent in many languages including some Indonesian dialects. As part of her field work, she'd lived in a tribal longhouse, deep in the Java jungle, sleeping at night with baskets of dried human skulls strung above her hammock. It was the first time a foreigner had visited and worked in that remote region.

I asked her what her most frightening experience had been. She took a long time to answer, there were many to consider:

"Maybe the time when a mixture of malaria and typhoid had a stranglehold on me. The elders of the tribe walked through dense jungle carrying me on a makeshift stretcher. When they finally reached a tiny airstrip I was whisked away in a light aircraft. I returned a week later".

I was looking quite aghast by the end of this tale but she turned to me and said,

"Well, what do you expect? I'm an anthropologist".

I wondered then what makes people so brave. What allows them to disregard their safety in the pursuit of knowledge. Here was a powerful woman, they were a formidable, inspiring couple.

As we said our goodbyes, she quietly said in my ear,

"You've got a gem of a daughter there". Praise indeed from an intrepid, fearless, courageous woman.

Nessie sits at a desk in a particularly stunning building set in the middle of dense jungle; surrounded by jogging paths, a central canteen, an Olympic-size swimming pool and exquisite tropical gardens. This is the headquarters of The Centre for International Forestry Research (CIFOR) - but Nessie does not work for them.

No one is quite sure how Nessie managed to commandeer this gorgeous working space, she had only once attended a workshop here. At that time, she was working in Jakarta in a tiny, concrete-lined office with no green spaces. The small NGO she works for didn't have its own offices. She was lonely and miserable, working on her own in a city where she knew no one. The NGO she works for has similar values and objectives to CIFOR and, somehow, she managed to wangle a desk here. So, there she sits each day and does her work, overjoyed to be here. The CIFOR staff seem bemused and uncertain why and what this young lady is doing here, but they love having her around.

People who work for NGOs tend to have lots in common. They are a resourceful bunch, sociable, tough, intense with big open faces and seem unafraid of almost anything. An Australian friend of Nessie's confided in me. She had felt "a bit rough" recently.

It transpired she had caught Dengue fever. The malaria she'd caught in Africa the year before had complicated matters. I found out her parents had been advised to come quickly and sit by her bedside. That was how ill she had been, but she could have been describing having a bad cold to me.

So, I was feeling a bit pathetic the next day surrounded by all these tough adventurers. That feeling would soon disappear. Nessie has joined The Bogor Hash House Harriers and was determined that we too would become part of it. A two-hour drive away, we arrived at the edge of another jungle in our track suits and trainers. Ness disappeared into the distance with the proper runners, abandoning Kenneth and I with the walking group. They were mostly local folk, so lots of smiling and pointing going on.

The rain wasn't coming down in sheets, it was more like vertical waterfalls. Later, when I looked at my face in a mirror it was streaked black. Great rivulets of mascara had run down my cheeks and my lipstick had morphed into unattractive lines down my chin but at that moment it didn't seem to matter.

We set off with a mixture of trepidation and enthusiasm and hadn't gone more than a few yards when I managed to slip into a paddy field. One leg mysteriously disappearing into the murky water, right up to the top of my thigh.

Lots of giggling all around me - certainly not by me. I almost breathed a sigh of relief misguidedly telling myself,

"I can turn back now, just go and sit in the car. Ness won't be cross. Kenneth can go on his own".

Just as this thought was materializing two tiny women snatched my hands, hauled me up and for the next few hours, guided me by the hand. We walked through tiny villages with open doors, through thick vegetation which sometimes had to be hewn down by our intrepid leader, a small man with the strength of a huge ox.

Part of the 'adventure' was having to follow the clues that had been set for us. I hadn't realised it was a game as well as a walk. Often, we would go wrong and end up retracing our steps. Throughout all of it everyone just chuckled. I found myself giggling, laughing like a wild person as I careered down steep passes oblivious to the various forms of creepy crawlies that had firmly attached themselves to me.

At one point, we tramped through a tiny settlement and the villagers came out to greet us. I could see them smiling and gesturing to the walkers ahead; then I appeared. Wedged-in between tiny ladies no higher than my elbows. There was I, a large pasty-faced creature being led along on this merry dance. They all clapped as I struggled past.

Sitting in the jeep on our way home, caked from head to toe in mud with bits of jungle still attached to me, I felt quite the adventurer, quite brave.

With love,

Angie

Dearest Ones,

A rather unnerving event happened a few days ago, so unnerving I'm getting a bit hot and bothered thinking about it, even so I'll carry on.

A few days ago, we said a tearful goodbye to Ness. She left for some distant island in Borneo. I knew there was no hospital, no air strip, just jungle and the threat of palm oil. I tried to forget about the journey she had to undertake. The two-hour taxi ride, two flights in tiny aeroplanes and an unstable canoe ride.

The conversation before she left seemed identical to all the other conversations we have had.

"Nessie just be careful and know how much I love you"

"Yes Ma, love you too and you know I'll be careful".

And then, " I won't have any mobile signal, I will be in the middle of a jungle so please don't worry (how well she knows me) if you don't hear from me for a while".

A few days later my mobile rings.

"Ma it's me. I can't talk for long, actually I'm just about to have a poo. I've got a wooden stick and I'll have to dig a hole soon. Just wanted to let you know all is fine, I love you" and with that she was gone, to dig her hole but with a brilliant mobile phone connection!

If I worried about her, or her brother, I'd be dead and buried by now something which I was quite convinced was just about to happen to me.........

Train tickets in our pockets, accommodation paid for, we were off, to Jogjakarta. There we were waiting on the doorstep early in the morning for our booked taxis. The taxis driver who had promised faithfully to arrive on time and now no trace of him and no other taxis to be found.

Yete, Nessie's housekeeper motioned to the motorbike which just happened to magically appear. Mr Rahman the gentleman who takes Nessie to work every morning (again one of those things I have to blot out of my mind) sat waiting patiently. Wearing a red and brown leather jacket which looked remarkably similar to his weather-beaten face. Nessie said he always seemed to appear just when you needed him. He stood and smiled through his remaining three and a half teeth. He carried on beaming waiting for something to happen, then suddenly said.

"Nessie's Mumma, I am here".

"There must be a mistake, we ordered a taxis Mr Rahman"

"No taxi, no taxi here, busy, you come with me Nessie's Mumma, here" indicating the back of the motorbike.

Trying hard not to raise my voice or betray the horror of the situation, I pleaded.

"No Mr Rahman, look at all our luggage, and all our bags and all our things and....."

I then started to panic and stared in disbelief. Surely, they can't expect me to get on that. I have a horror of motorbikes. As a teenager I left home one night, telling my parents I was "just going around the corner". A thirty-minute train ride away, I had an assignation, with a boy and his Lambretta. The boy started to show off, having just acquired the bike, illegally having a daft passenger, me, on the back. He careered around a corner at high speed, came off and I stayed on, but not for long. We ended up in hospital. I still have a rather nasty scar on my knee and the memories of the police terrifying us. Those memories came flooding back as I stood looking at Mr Rahman's massive motorbike.

Kenneth was looking very thoughtful, then shrugged his shoulders and got onto the other motorbike, which again mysteriously seemed to appear. I then lurched towards this damn machine, hitched up my patterned flowered tea dress and clambered on, along with; a 25kg suitcase, a backpack, a straw hat, my oversized travelling cashmere shawl, plus an assortment of needed carrier bags, which contained little snacks and drinks for our journey.

I didn't just cling to him; I didn't look like the other pillion passengers who nonchalantly sit on the back watching the scenery. No, that poor man. I grabbed his sides and clamped my entire body around him, not easy when the huge suitcase was between us. He will have my fingerprints engraved on his person forever.

Indonesian traffic is horrific and rush hour traffic is the worst. Hundreds but hundreds of motorbikes, vehicles that look like they've been thrown together with a couple of wheels randomly attached, compete with ugly great cars brandishing bull bars on the front. Everyone drives totally unaware of anything else that might be on the roads; school children, dogs, men and women rushing to work, street venders, unwitting tourists, all weave their precarious way through this madness. The noise is deafening, everyone loves the sound of their horns and motorbike engines explode, adding to the mayhem.

We skirted within inches of other vehicles, I could easily have reached out and touched them all as we brushed past them. All the time my dress was riding higher and higher up my body, by the time we get to the station it's around my waist, but I don't care. By now I'm so deliriously happy to be still alive. I grabbed my motorbike hero and started kissing him. He was overcome possibly by the pain in his ribs I'd inflicted, or maybe because no stranger has ever tried to kiss him quite so enthusiastically before.

"Nessie's Mumma, new experience"

I wasn't sure how to answer that.

"You come back soon, again, a bike ride?". Although as he said this, I got the feeling he was not really looking forward to another tortuous journey.

I make myself look animated, thanked him again knowing I would never go near another motorbike ever again.

He departed with a peculiar expression on his face. I can't quite work out whether he was happy or deeply relieved, but I'm sure he's going to be very sympathetic with Ness when he sees her next time. Her mother is of the hysterical kind.

Kenneth arrived 10 mins later with the bigger suitcase, an assortment of bags and his panama hat intact, still sat firmly on his head and we ran for our train.

With love,

Angie

Hello Everyone,

I promise faithfully and will endeavour not to be one of those ghastly mothers who boast about their children: there is nothing worse. I will be careful and attempt not to bore the pants off you. But I do know that many of you want to hear how the first screening of Guy's short film, Overview, went. So, with a huge amount of pride, here we go.

Middle of the night, jetlag kicked in. Slowly, I made my way to the kitchen. A light was burning, someone must had forgotten to turn it off. But no, there was Guy, head bent over a mountain of papers, scribbling away.

Keep calm I told myself, don't look worried, don't say anything that might be cause for concern and for God's sake don't say…
…"why didn't you do this before now?"

I continued repeating this to myself, like a senseless mantra, while he informed me that he was writing his presentation. That day, that very day, a five hundred-seater theatre would be packed. Many eminent, distinguished, brilliant brains would come to listen to him.

I summed up as much grace as I could manage, smiled and made a cup of camomile tea. As I made my weary way out of the room, a voice behind me called out,

"Don't worry Ma, it's all in hand" - and it was.

We were visiting one of America's oldest and most prestigious universities. It is littered with past presidents of the USA; eight of them were students here. Many Nobel Laureates and Pulitzer prize winners were spawned here along with Olympic athletes. The place pulses with wealth, privilege and brilliant brains.

Magnificent towering colonial-style memorial halls; mansion houses accommodating elite students, gorgeous Georgian gate houses and all of them built in red, earthy brick which oozes old money and refinement, manicured lawns with lavish flower borders are everywhere.

Reality kicked in for Kenneth and me when we arrived at the university. There, a long line of excited looking people was waiting to enter the theatre.

Guy, Steve and Christophe's, 20-minute film Overview was shown and as the closing credits rolled the theatre erupted with applause. The clapping continued as Guy took his place on the stage for a Question-and-Answer session. He sat in the middle of a collection of the most inspiring, indomitable, brave men imaginable. I've gone and Googled them all, here's a little snapshot of them.:

Frank White the brilliant writer, philosopher and teacher, wrote the book The Overview Effect, which describes the shift in awareness that results from looking at the Earth from space. It profoundly affects space travellers' views of themselves and the planet they inhabit. Guy and Steve, as fifteen-year-old rebellious, discontented schoolboys were inspired. There and then, vowed they would make a film that would do justice to this book. Frank believes it does.

Jeff Hoffman, a doctor of astrophysics and a walker in space. He was one of the astronauts responsible for repairing parts of the Hubble space telescope. He has notched up over a thousand hours in space.

Doug Trumbull, a film maker, a visual effects pioneer responsible for visual effects in films like Blade Runner - and an inventor. Nominated for an Oscar.

Ron Garan, a former USAF test and fighter pilot who accomplished two space missions aboard the International Space Station, spending over a hundred and seventy days in space and including four 'space-walks'.

......and then, there's Guy.

Pride in a child is a tricky thing; it's quite easy to let it reflect back on the parents. But I did feel unbelievably proud: I probably looked like a blown-up peacock. There he was, on stage, seated amongst a panel of world-class scientists, astronauts, and philosophers seeming as though this was an everyday occurrence.

Like his film, Overview, Guy was quite awe inspiring.

Enough, before I start squawking just like a peacock.

Sending love - and do watch the film. This quote from an Apollo 8 astronaut sort of sums up this beautiful and breath-taking short film,

"We came all this way to explore the moon and the most important thing that we discovered was ...Earth".

With love,

Angie

I'm watching our small army of ants hurriedly weaving backwards and forwards from the table. Those wayward crumbs that escaped the dustpan and brush are now travelling up the walls of bamboo, to a place in the roof.

We share the house with them along with dragon flies and various sized spiders - some as big as your hand (but it's the tiny ones that nip). Big, fat, stripy hornets lay their eggs just above our bed in a most elaborately constructed nest. It hangs precariously on the wall like a rustic sculpture. We watch the hornets carry little live morsels of food to feed their young, who have been laid inside another live insect, which is slowly being eaten away from the inside. Macabre and strangely fascinating.

I mustn't forget the gecko; how could I? A very vocal one.

Each day around teatime he makes his presence known. He hurries out, positions himself in the same place on the ceiling and lets out a loud croak. I like to fantasise, thinking he's letting us know he's in charge and looking after us. Geckos eat all the nasties.

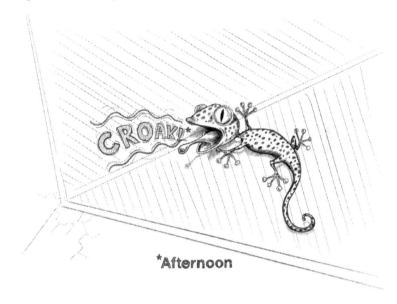

CROAK!

*Afternoon

Last night, as we sat on the tiny terrace, fireflies danced among the fields. Nessie tells us they are an endangered species because of all the light pollution but here in the paddy fields they glimmered and glowed, our own magic light show.

If I were being generous, the house could be described as basic. 'Rustic' would be the word used if Mr Londo had a marketing manager; he does not. He deals with tourists in the most bad-tempered and cantankerous manner imaginable. I was trying, unsuccessfully, to negotiate the rent and our length of stay. Then, Nessie arrived. He scowled horribly as she came up the garden path. Another of those tourists trying to 'find themselves'. This is Ubud, after all, full of yoga, crystal reading, navel gazing and everything else you could think of associated with 'finding your inner child'.

So, there is Mr Londo his face turning even more sour until the moment Nessie opens her mouth. This lovely young woman starts chatting to Mr Londo not in English, but in Indonesian. His mouth began to move, and suddenly, a huge smile engulfed his weathered, now pleasant, nut-brown face. We're sorted.

The move here from our hotel did not go smoothly. We seemed to have acquired a huge assortment of bags and suitcases; all of Nessie's worldly goods. She has said goodbye to her life in Java and is now starting an intensive yoga teacher-training course - and we are here as the support team.

The move would have been more manageable if the house we've decided to call home for a while wasn't up at least eighty steep, slippery, moss-clad, uneven steps high up on the side of a hill. The community here seems suspended above everything else. A secret collection of huts, homes and paddy fields. We had to recruit a band of local folk, as helpers, and I was certain they would suffer heart attacks or collapse in the middle of the journey. But we made it and have settled in nicely and it really does feel like home.

This wooden house, on stilts, sits bang in the middle of a paddy field. A tiny little path, the width of a foot, leads you to the front door. We might be lucky enough to be here for a complete growing and harvesting cycle of the rice. Wiry men, whose skin has turned the colour of dark caramel, tend the fields as the sun beats down on them every day. They wear thin cotton clothes and raffia hats that look like small pyramids. They smile and greet us every day with grace and gentleness. Even when shooing away the ill-disciplined ducks who waddle around like a band of Sergeant Majors, these men retain their serenity. I long to strike up a conversation but smiles and kind gestures have to suffice. The other day, a big fat pineapple was left on the porch. There were extra smiles and gestures from one of the men.

Downstairs is the kitchen. Two wobbly gas rings and the oddest collection of kitchen utensils I have ever seen. Mismatched plates, lots of egg cups, a garlic press with the press bit missing, tiny glasses impossible to drink out of, pots and pans, some so badly bashed they are unstable on the cooker. I suspect there might also be a collection of large spiders but I refuse to look for evidence.

Upstairs is the bedroom; one huge room with magnificent views in every direction across the paddy fields. The windows have no glass; the breeze blows through.

I have to use a bucket to go for a wee wee at night as Kenneth is sure I would break my neck falling down the rickety steep stairs. I would probably be sure to meet the spiders, as large as dinner plates, who would also be vying for the loo.

I had to scrub the very mucky kitchen and the bathroom on moving in. Mr Londo offered the services of a cleaner. That's a good idea I thought. He hurried up the path shortly returning clutching a grey and very suspect moth-eaten mop. It turns out he's the cleaner. I haven't the heart to stop him. As I write this, I can hear him happily mopping away and I'm thinking I will have to re-do everything that horrid, manky mop has touched. But I feel Mr Londo is going to prove to be a very interesting character. I'm really looking forward to getting to know him.

Have to go now: a rather large insect has settled on the desk where I am writing and looks like he's up to no good.

With love,

Angie

to:	family and friends
from:	Joyful Traveller
subject:	Bali, Indonesia - Mr. Londo

Me and Mr. Londo have been hanging out together. It seems there is more to my landlord than meets the eye. What's that old expression? 'never judge a book by its cover'. In this case, it is entirely true.

His usual outfit is a well-worn grubby vest and little shorts that flap around his painfully thin legs. But when he spies me coming up his garden path he promptly scurries into his shed, and emerges wearing a less grubby tee shirt. I've now learnt to walk a little slower to his hut, to give him time to change. This allows him to emerge looking quite important, ready for our daily get-togethers. He continues to regard me in a bemused and comical manner. This over-large, red head who sits on his steps and bombards him with many questions.

I have to reign in my curiosity and tread carefully. I do not want to offend this gentleman. I am aware of how valuable and unique these encounters are. So, there we sit on the ancient steps which have been worn to a sliver, dangerously unstable. We sit in the sun together chatting while flocks of ducks waddle past. They, too, look very important. Such bossy birds and so full of themselves. They take no notice of us and continue on their journey looking earnest and serious while Mr. Londo and I keep chatting. It's very gentle. We are getting to know each other. We sort of pass the time of day and with each encounter I learn a little more about this fascinating man.

I was smiling to myself as I sat on the steps remembering how frightfully sullen and crabby Mr. Londo was only a week ago.

He started laughing and I felt much delight. As he laughed, I could see, nestled in his mouth, a collection of the most terrible brown teeth. His face is worn, like old shoe leather, but his smile wakes up his eyes and he takes on the air of a little boy. I told him about my encounter with the spider who lives in the kitchen, the size of a dinner plate. How I had been trapped, for over an hour waiting for him to run back to his nest in the ceiling. He rolled around, slapping his thighs. The idea of me pinned to the ground behind the table, unable to move because of a spider, obviously appealed to his sense of humour.

Mr. Londo was a poor farmer scratching out a living in the forests behind our house. From what I gather, he never went to school and still can't read or write but what he can do - is paint. He paints these magical, highly coloured scenes of Balinese life. Nothing seems left out. The gods, the rituals, the ancestors, the legends all are weaved together on these funny odd canvases.

It all started with this man, Arie Smit - a well-known Dutch painter. He was incarcerated in a Japanese prisoner-of-war camp and after the war ended found it impossible to return to Holland and his old life so he settled in Bali. While he roamed the fields, he noticed numerous young men working there. He dished out many boxes of paints and canvases and waited. His wait was not in vain. There amongst the rice paddies, the jungle and the fields lurked some talented young men. Mr. Londo was one of these young men. He had never seen a paint brush, let alone pick one up and use it, but it emerged that he had a talent.

I then find out that Mr. Londo has not one, but four houses that he rents out. By Balinese standards, he is a wealthy man. And he's travelled to Australia and various parts of Asia. But, and this is quite extraordinary, Mr. Londo has chosen to live in a tiny wooden shed up our garden path where the walls are covered with his paintings. A kitchen at the rear with a single gas hob sits alongside a piece of furniture that looks like a large child's crib. The only other item is a hefty, rickety wooden table that takes up most of the space. There, placed in meticulous order, are coloured pencils and tubes of paint and cups of tea that Mr. Londo has forgotten to drink. I'm still unsure of the whereabouts of the washing and lavatory facilities.

He especially likes Kenneth. He watches him with great enjoyment as he emerges from the overgrown paths. Most days, Kenneth goes shopping, returning laden down with various household items; new mugs, a kettle, kitchen rolls and a mop. Now, when we have a shower, we won't slip and crack our heads on the bathroom tiles which undulate madly as you stand on them. We really are all set up.

Think I spied Mrs Londo today doing a bit of sweeping outside. "She certainly doesn't live there". Kenneth remarked, "he's got it made, his own shed and no one to bother him".

I replied, "I've got an idea, when we get back to Bristol you could erect your own shed on our allotment and live there in the summer months".

With love,

Angie

to: family and friends

from: Joyful Traveller

subject: Bali, Indonesia - Before the Day of Silence

Hello Everyone,

Tomorrow is Nyepi, The Day of Silence.

But tonight is the Saka New Year's Eve. Families start the evening with blessings at the family temple. In Bali, as many as five generations live together. A stone wall surrounds an assortment of houses, kitchens, store cupboards for rice, compounds for pigs and the important family temple. When a son marries, he stays, and his wife joins him in the family compound.

On this night, each member of the family participates in chasing away malevolent forces from their homes. Pots and pans and anything else that makes a loud banging noise, are struck repeatedly together with a fiery bamboo torch.

The spirits are later manifested as Ogoh-Ogohs, gigantic, gruesome looking wooden effigies. Even the name could send shivers down your spine. These are paraded through the streets. Evil spirits are enticed with the most delicious and complicated of offerings, and every conceivable noise-making instrument known to mankind is used to frighten them away. The louder the noise, the quicker the spirits will flee.

No one is left in their home. All are out on the streets watching, parading, tugging children by the hand. The elderly or infirm who can't walk are bounced around in their wheelchairs. Everyone has to be there.

The colours are frantic, overpowering. Everywhere you look there are flowers and faces lit up by oil lamps. High above, lanterns burn, and the gamelans and drums compete with each other in a crazy alliance. We followed the crowds. I was giddy with delight, not wanting to miss a moment, and all around us smiling faces, happy we were there in the throng, part of it all.

Tonight, these effigies, representing evil spirits which are believed to have brought disease and misery to the island this year, will be set on fire, in the belief that the flames will cleanse the island and the evil spirits will leave.

At 6am tomorrow morning the silence will begin.

The airport closes for 24 hours - not one plane is allowed to arrive or depart. This is the only place in the world where this occurs. Empty streets are patrolled by special security men recruited by the village elders, to make sure no one leaves their home. Tourists stay tightly shut up in their hotels. Lights can only be used by foreigners if they are unseen from the road. Children learn from an early age how special this day is and honour it.

We will behave as the Balinese do. Stocked up on cold food and emergency torches at the ready. The Scotsman looks rather happy at the prospect of complete silence, no talking from me for 24 hours

Next day the Balinese will meet family and friends and ask for forgiveness from each other. I fear my list might be quite long.

With love,

Angie

The Day of Silence is over. It felt as though the whole world was at peace. The island was completely silent, not even all those scabby dogs barked. I suppose they had no one to bark at.

Everyone was part of this extraordinary day. We heard no voices, no cars, no alarms, no motorbikes, no aeroplanes - just the cacophony of wildlife, louder than ever. That night, sitting on our terrace looking over the paddy fields, only the flickering of candlelight and the fireflies performing their waltzes in the skies could been seen.

Today is the first day of the Balinese New Year and all that silent, peaceful energy seems to have made the Balinese smiles even broader. I know there are problems on this beautiful island - I'm not that naïve - but it feels to me as though there is a longing to heal, themselves, the environment, and the wider world. As a kind and wise taxi driver explained to me,

"We think of our families, we think of our communities, we think of our ancestors and we pray for the world".

Today is the day that each Balinese will ask forgiveness from family and friends and be eternally grateful for all the good things in their lives. I'm just feeling grateful and humble that I've managed to keep your friendships, even though I can be such a pain at times.

When we eventually leave this magical island, we have to go back home via Hong Kong. If I end up in the jump seat as a toilet monitor again, I won't mind in the slightest, because I'm going to try to be like most of the folks here, graceful and grateful.

With love,

Angie

Here we are in this tiny Balinese village on the edge of Ubud. Ubud is a town known for its yoga, lentil munching and its vegan-sandal-wearing community. Chilled out and very Om; sit in the lotus position and breathe deeply. I've started attending yoga classes. Held in a huge wooden house on stilts, glassless windows open out onto the paddy fields. A heady combination of incense and frangipani fills the air. Rust-coloured dragon flies, huge velvet butterflies - dark as night - and bird-song competing with croaking frogs. It's all so glorious, so extravagant, so utterly beautiful. This is indeed paradise but even in paradise things are not perfect. The Scotsman caught a tummy bug, now on the road to recovery, at least half a stone lighter. I don't think our kitchen is all that hygienic. I'm now certain there might be a rat or two, lurking in the broken-down cupboards. We've taken to stamp our feet, heavily before we enter.

I emerge from my class and sit in the nearby café. A magical place made of bamboo and intricately carved wood. Open to the elements, there's a gentle breeze that blows through the place adding to the exquisite sense of calm. While I sip my 'Eternal Life Youth Elixir Antioxidant Immune Boosting' beverage, I become aware of a lady sitting along the bench from me. I am being observed.

She is the same lady I noticed in the class. She didn't actually look at me as we were doing our 'Downward Dogs', it was more that she made her presence felt. She had short, cropped hair and a body honed to perfection by years of yoga. She's a no-nonsense Dutch lady who lives here. We chat away until she comes to the part where she tells me what she does for a living. She's a Family Constellation Therapist, she heals families' energy. I'm not quite sure what exactly it is she does, so I ask her for an example.

"There are hundreds" she says, "but I'll give you one situation". She looks at me with a gentle intensity,

"Suppose you have twins in the womb. Suppose one dies as it leaves the mother's body. Say, a boy – who dies and the other baby, a girl - who lives". She turns away.

I start to feel sick, an ache from the depths of my being rises to the surface. I'm shaking and I say,

"But that's me. I'm that baby who survived".

She doesn't reply, but gently smiles and gets up to leave. As she does, she takes my hand and tells me that all is well, that he is at peace and from now on, I should be too. I just need to light a candle and acknowledge him.

That night, I do exactly that. I stop worrying and wondering how on earth she could have known my story; how could she have? I'm still intensely curious but it has brought me a great sense of peace and, yes, I do believe this twin of mine is at peace. It was like finding the missing piece of a jigsaw. Something had mended.

It's part of life here in this deeply spiritual, achingly beautiful land, with its connection to its ancestors.

Every morning, the Balinese set out offerings to the Gods. Some are tiny parcels made out of palm leaves, little bits of coconut, tiny fragments of flowers - all lovingly put together. Others are larger more elaborate creations but all of them have one thing in common; to give thanks and praise to their Gods,

"We're so grateful we're not living in a part of the world where there is not enough food to go around" said the taxi driver. I seem to be learning so much from taxi drivers here. This feeling of gratitude and gratefulness permeates everything, it's infectious.

Ceremonies are part of everyday life. Last night, walking into town down a dark unlit path we suddenly had to stand aside as a long procession snaked past us. Joy and happiness bouncing from all who were taking part. Beating tambourines, vibrating drums, intriguing-looking musical instruments, all played with delight and every face with a smile.

Ness can now hold a conversation in Indonesian. When she opens her mouth and starts talking the Balinese are surprised and intrigued.

Sitting in the back of a taxi the other day, Nessie stops midway in conversation with me and starts a conversation in Indonesian with the driver. I could see his face in the mirror. It was as though he'd been slapped hard and didn't understand where it had come from. He said nothing and quickly steered his taxi to the side of the road. He still didn't turn around but looked with great suspicion in his rear-view mirror, straining to see who was in the back of the car. Later, he told us he believed in spirits and ancestors returning to communicate. He was relieved and amazed when he found out the words were coming from Nessie's mouth. After that they had a cheerful conversation together.

Some of you lovely lot have written, worried about the earthquake. Please don't worry. No one here seems bothered by the odd earthquake - erupting volcanos are much more pressing. Today, we travel to a small village on the coast for a few days recommended by a friend of Nessie's. An isolated little bay with a couple of shacks for surfers. Ness could easily be taken for a surfer - but Kenneth and I ...not. I'm just going to dream.

Many Blessings (as they say here) to you all.

With love,

Angie

to: family and friends

from: Joyful Traveller

subject: Denpasar, Bali, Indonesia - The International Hospital

Dear Ones,

You know that feeling when you feel sorry for yourself? It's a bit rubbish but in the bigger picture this is not so bad. It could have been much worse.

Yesterday morning, while clambering out of the swimming pool, I tumbled in an undignified manner landing heavily on my wrist. I am now the proud owner of a metal plate and six screws bolted into my wrist covered by a rather violent scar.

I was operated on in the late afternoon. The journey down to the hospital theatre was a surreal affair. Flat on my back and in considerable pain, we seemed to trundle on for mile after mile. Two gentle-faced Balinese hospital porters smiled benignly down at me. They spoke no English, but I could tell they were probably lovely with their mothers. One stroked my shoulder when I tried to raise my head. We just seemed to carry on getting deeper and deeper into the bowels of this hospital. I had no idea if the surgeon carrying out this rather delicate operation was at all competent. Would I go under and never emerge from the general anaesthetic?

Last night, after all the hardware had been installed and I came round from the anaesthetic, I experienced a rather miserable spell. Kenneth couldn't wait to escape back to the house. He was valiantly trying to disguise his horror of anything remotely medical. When he started shifting his weight agitatedly from one side to another, looking like a little boy desperate to have a pee, I suggested he leave, which he did, promptly - his pallid face retreating out of the door.

Usually, the kindest and caring of men but he does have serious issues with hospitals. In the middle of Nessie's birth, I thought he was going to keel over and flatten me, as did the midwives. They appeared far more concerned about him than me, asking him often how HE was. I have a vague recollection of him being brought a cup of tea and a couple of rich tea biscuits.

Nessie had huge amounts of homework and had been with me all day, so I insisted she leave too. The doctor kindly prescribed me a big dose of pain killers and I drifted off into a disturbed sleep.

The nurses are a joy. Sometimes I want to ring my bell just so I can see them. They tend to come into the room in pairs. Tiny creatures, who remind me of hummingbirds. They move purposely and with speed but still retain a grace and dignity in whatever they are doing. Their uniforms are a brilliant white. Do they ever sit down? there is never a hint of a crease in those dazzling dresses. Even at the end of a long shift they look as though they have just put their uniforms on straight out of the laundry.

They seem captivated by my red hair. I don't let on and tell them it's out of a bottle. I feel a bit like Gulliver in Lilliput. I reckon I am twice the size of them and if I have to get up for a little walk, they insist on positioning themselves either side of me. I tower like a giant next to them. My feet, which I've always thought were on the dainty side for my height, are like great ungainly plates of meat next to theirs.

They are kind and considerate and I can't imagine any of them being bad-tempered. They have shown me boundless photos of their children, parents, siblings, friends, their houses, the birds they keep in cages, festival celebrations - these are all shown to me with great excitement and happiness,

"On your departure, Madam, may many photos be taken?".

When I agreed, they seemed to smile even wider.

Good news. It's my third night in hospital and I've just seen the surgeon. He said I was a model patient and he's thrilled with his handiwork. I'm allowed to leave tomorrow with lots of strong pain killers and a huge packet of antibiotics. They seem to be a bit paranoid about foreigners catching infections. It was hilarious listening to Nessie arguing, she didn't think I needed them, the doctors won.

"You have a very forceful daughter Mrs Reid, one who needs to be complimented on", the charming anaesthetist said. He was an amusing and sociable man who would often stop by for a little chat. He loved talking English and he had a captive audience in Nessie and me.

"You are an athlete Mrs Reid". Nessie almost fell out of her chair. This was said before the operation. I have always had low blood pressure and a slow pulse, so he assumed I was super fit.

I keep thinking it could have been so much worse. Waiting in the emergency room, a very beautiful, chic French woman was lying on a trolley next to me. I noticed her because she was wearing the most gorgeous array of linen clothes. The sort only the very slim with a yoga-honed body could possibly wear. While I was admiring her clothes I tried to strike up a conversation. I thought I could even ask her, politely, where her outfit was from but she was distraught; she wouldn't even look at me. They came to wheel her away and I later found out from the surgeon that she had broken her hip badly and was on her way back to France. I then realised how lucky I was to have only broken a wrist.

Forgot to mention, the surgeon looked like something out of a movie, told me he loved my accent.

Look, I can even type!

Much love,

Angie

Dear Ones,

The beautiful man was sitting ramrod straight on his meditation cushion. His jet-black hair hung like a thick curtain. His body honed by years of yoga was encased in muscles that rippled as he moved. His face was angelic. He came from a long line of yogis. He was born with the wisdom of his ancestors coursing through his veins. He was exceptional - and prepared to teach me how to meditate.

Two weeks earlier I had pranced lightly into his meditation room. I started to tell him my plans. I had so many plans: I would walk for miles every day, I would explore the island on a bicycle, I would have a yoga practice every day, I would swim and snorkel, I would learn to cook Balinese dishes. Oh, and I would do some English teaching. Yes, I had everything worked out.

This time I arrived with fingers and a thumb sticking out of a hefty cast, the metal plate in my wrist with its six screws needed to be held securely in place.

As I approached him, I began to feel very sorry for myself. He started to laugh. More uncontrollable laughter gripped his body and with that he fell off his plump cushion. I stood there completely bewildered watching this mad man laughing and then I, too, started to laugh. The absurdity of it all suddenly dawned on me. All those schemes and plans I had, all that feeling of being in control. Later, he told me how much the Gods must have laughed while I had made my plans a few weeks before.

I told him his English needed some improving,

"then teach me", he retorted.

He's coming on Monday for his first lesson. At least one of my plans has been realised.

With love,

Angie

to: family and friends

from: Joyful Traveller

subject: Bali, Indonesia - Teaching and green snakes

The yogi arrived, intrigued by our wobbly house in the middle of a paddy field. I think he might have been expecting some rather chi-chi designer pad, all soft green paintwork and open-plan. The ducks even made an appearance, marching within touching distance with their waddling gait and superior attitude, pecking at their fellow unfortunates if they didn't keep up. Some definite thugs in this line-up.

The worn-out table on the worn-out veranda is set at an awkward angle. One of the legs looks like ants have had a good meal from it. The chairs creak alarmingly and sway if you move too suddenly, but we settle in. My yogi, looking bemused and cheerful, turns out to be an exemplary student. He repeats, with concentration and fluency the phrases which I think will come in handy in his work.

He has this overwhelming calmness about him. His movements are like slow-flowing water. Grace and a deep sense of contentment are transferred, for a little while onto me. After the lesson we sit in silence. As night draws in the fireflies emerge, dancing in the dark. Then, sounds from the paddy fields start to fill the air; frogs croaking manically - all madly competing with one another and armies of crickets with their frantic, high-pitched screech, reminiscent of someone running their thumb down the teeth of a comb. They are busy advertising themselves, look at me they say, then tell any competitors within earshot to beat it.

As my student prepares to leave, he instructs me to be watchful of snakes. I tell him of my encounters.

There are thirty-five different species of snakes including six highly venomous ones in Bali. The venomous ones are the killers, if you don't seek medical help immediately, you're a goner. The Island

Pit Viper is widespread and lives in trees and bushes and loves to come out at night and party. Incredible as it seems, the café we visit almost every day has a resident guest living in one of its trees. The owner assured us he won't come out in the daytime. When I pointed out to him that we often come for supper he just sort of shrugged his shoulders. I saw him the other day - the viper that is - a bright green thing, about 3-feet long, with a wide arrow-shaped head and beady red eyes.

Last week we were ambling along a narrow lane with a high stone wall on one side, a paddy field on the other. A group of animated teenagers stopped our progress, desperate to point out something but very anxious we should not venture near it. The little group of youngsters were trying their best to be brave, considerate and appear as though they were in control, but they were obviously a bit scared. There, on the wall a few feet up from the path was a deadly Island Pit Viper. The narrow path would have allowed the snake to take a lethal bite at an unsuspecting passer-by.

The 'snake man' had been called; all we needed to do was to wait. A little crowd had gathered, every eye glued to the snake. An older gentleman silently weaved his way through the crowd. He carried an ancient wooden stick with a deadly looking spike on the end. An almost kung-fu type action saw his stick leap out of his hand impaling the snake and dropping it to the ground where it writhed in its death throes.

He slowly and cautiously approached the snake and then, after another well aimed jab to the head, he appeared satisfied. Another nifty movement and the snake was deposited into the sack that was wrapped around his shoulders.

In an ideal world, this poor snake should have been left alone without everybody crowding in on its territory, invading its home.

However, any feelings of sadness for the fate of this snake quickly evaporated when I remembered what would happen to one of its unfortunate victims. Human tissue is rapidly eaten away at the site of the bite. This leads to internal bleeding, skin blackening and, if in a limb and not treated, amputation. There is no anti-venom but the hospital in the capital, Denpasar, does have a special ward where snake bites are treated.

According to my yogi, if Kenneth and I ever get bitten by a snake we are to take ourselves off, pretty sharpish, to a local healer - a Balian. They have century-old cures, even the local conventional doctors have been heard whispering to concerned tourists, "get yourself to the Balian".

"How would I know where to find one?"

"Everyone knows where the local Balian is".

Getting into bed that night after doing our inspection rounds for snakes, spiders, scorpions and generally eyeing up any other creatures that we share this space with, I felt a little safer, knowing that a Balian will be somewhere nearby.

With love,

Angie

to: family and friends

from: Joyful Traveller

subject: Bali, Indonesia - A Visit to a Balian

Hello Everyone,

After our English lesson my yogi announces,

"It is time for the Balian".

A Balian is a traditional healer, and each village has at least four of them. There are over 8,000 of them on this magical island. For many Balinese, their first medical choice would be a Balian. Misguided missionaries called them all manner of names; witch doctors, magic men, snake oil users. But now, it's said that even Western trained doctors, with all their swanky hospitals and complicated procedures, sometimes whisper in their patients' ears, "better go to the Balian" if their patients are not making a satisfactory recovery.

We are well out of town, deep in the paddy fields. Women are carrying heavy bundles of various things on their heads, firewood, bricks, water bottles. Ancient men walk by their skin deeply furrowed, wrinkles overpowering their faces. It's so hot and humid the sweat runs down our noses and settles on our clothes.

The taxi pulls up, a gate grinds open and there in front of us is a pretty, cultivated garden complete with English pink and white roses, deep purple violas and bright orange nasturtiums. It's so surprising, we could be in my father's garden back home in Bristol. The small house has a wraparound veranda complete with a couple of wooden rocking chairs.

There I am with these pudgy fingers sticking out of bandages that have taken on a worn, scabby look. It's impossible to move any of them, or my overblown fat thumb which throbs spasmodically with pain.

As we emerged from the car, all I could hear was this strident voice. In that moment, I am transported back to my girls' school, and I swear I am hearing the voice of the fiercely organised head girl who used to drive all of us wayward pupils bonkers.

After she had finished with the taxi driver she turned her attention to Kenneth and me, directing us to seats on the veranda and then traipsed off. It was all so surreal and odd. If she'd brought back fine English bone china teacups complete with Earl Grey tea and maybe some pink fancies, I wouldn't have batted an eye lid. But it was only water she offered, commanding us to, "drink it all down".

Diana was wearing a skirt that looked decidedly Laura Ashley, with a sensible shirt. I'm being a bit mean here, but she did a little, remind me of a horse. I remembered when I was at drama school one of the dippy exercises we had to do was to think of an animal we thought our partner looked like - and proceed to act like it. My partner - not a particularly pleasant person - told me I resembled a Red Setter because they were neurotic creatures - all over the place - and not very bright. She didn't actually say out loud the last bit about being not very bright, but I could tell that was what she was thinking.

Diana had great big teeth, no idea how old she might be, parents live in the Home Counties. Diana definitely has a past; 'bit of a good time girl', Kenneth thought.

We were sipping our water, trying to look relaxed when the healer suddenly appeared like a being from another world. He was wearing a tiny vest and flimsy linen yoga trousers. His arm muscles bulged out of his vest like coiled snakes. His face was beautiful; mahogany skin and long wiry hair which cascaded down his back like a slow waterfall. His smile creased up his entire face; you just wanted to smile back at him, which I found myself doing constantly.

We sat very comfortably in the shade. A bit of chit-chatting went on. He spoke no English but Diana was an expert interpreter. As she translated back and forth, I got a glimpse of this woman.

A kind one, a caring one, one that believed passionately in her partner's gifts. I started to like her immensely and yet again chastise myself for being so judgemental on first impressions.

They examined my arm. He turned his head from side to side sighing deeply, unhappy the hospital hadn't given me a sling to wear. My fingers were stiff and bloated, and now my poor broken wrist was starting to throb with pain.

I watched his back as I followed him. It reminded me of the diagrams you get in osteopaths consulting rooms, where the skin is left off and all you see are the exposed muscles. I thought one quick chop of his hand and he could kill a person. He indicated towards a red-bricked building and then moved round to my side, gently holding my left arm we walked together across the courtyard. I suppose I might have been a bit fearful at this juncture, but I wasn't.

It is not unlike a temple, a sacred space where the healing happens. Along one wall is a shrine where Hindu Gods appear, carved from out of the wall. Lots of them; richly coloured, fierce, compassionate, benign and happy. Incense burned and candles flickered in the dim light.

He indicted a mat on the floor where I lay down. He stood in front of his shrine with me lying on the mat squinting at him through half closed eyes. The Balian stood there and didn't move a muscle. He stood, and before my eyes, turned into what resembled a magnificent marble statue. There was no sign of breathing, how long this went on for I don't know. I became mesmerised. The shadows cast by the candles and the wafts of incense seemed to blur into one another.

The room was bathed in peace, dripping from the very walls. It came to settle on me and I felt a huge release, but it didn't last long.

He sprinkled me with the water that had been sitting on the altar. I'm then given the most powerful, the most painful massage that I have ever had in the whole of my life. I made all these horrible noises. I sounded a bit like a pig, grunting and snorting. I yelped like a dog hoping he would hear me, hoping he'd understand my pain, but he carried on oblivious to my moans.

Eventually, he wrenched me up into a sitting position. He then sat behind me and reached under my right arm touching a point, and all I could think of is that he had electrocuted me. A huge current went down my arm with tremendous force and left through my thumb. I was so shocked I could hardly breath. I tried to look for the electric probe he must have used, but there wasn't one. He rose, sprinkled more water on to my head, prayed over me and opened the door.

I emerged into the daylight in a trance-like state and took my place again on the veranda. There, Kenneth looked relieved when he saw me still in one piece. Diana appeared as if by magic and animatedly pointed to my fingers.

I looked down to where those limp, white, bloated little sausages had been and in their place were pink fingers and a thumb that can now move freely. No pain.

My wrist has started to mend; The Gods and the Balian have worked their magic.

With love,

Angie

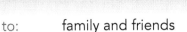

to: family and friends

from: Joyful Traveller

subject: Chiang Mai, Thailand 2014 - Chiang Mai, monks and street traders.

Hello Everyone,

After Guy came off his scooter and broke his leg Kenneth hopped on a standby flight and rushed out to be with him. Telling no one of his plans he arrived in Chiang Mai at the guest house where Guy was staying. Christoph, Guy's great friend and business partner, fortunately has a strong heart. Apparently, he leapt into the air when he entered Guy's room, looking frantically from Guy to Kenneth and back many times, not sure if he was seeing an apparition. There was Kenneth sat on Guy's bed as if he had been there the whole time. I think Guy secretly was expecting this amazing father of his to just appear without any warning, and, he did.

This city seemed the perfect place to finish the film, cheaper than New York where Guy was living and, similarly, London where Christoph was. Steve was back in Bristol completing the editing. Perfect - apart from a badly broken leg. This was a couple of months ago, and here we are now.

Kenneth back for a second time, this time with me trying not to fuss over Guy and his broken leg. It helps as I have an ally here in the form of Guy's lovely American girlfriend, Blaire. When I start to worry, she gently steers me away, a comforting and wise presence.

Chiang Mai is set in a beautiful part of Northern Thailand, a serene and laid-back city, unlike the madness of Bangkok. Barefoot monks collect alms in the mornings then it's the turn of the street traders at night. Everyone seems to rub along together very happily. It's a city that is rapidly changing but the old way of life still seems to be embraced by the young, especially where food is concerned. Traditional shops and street food traders are everywhere.

Food is important and respected even in the simplest of places. We sit at pavement cafés and eat delicious food prepared right in front of us. Old oil drums grilling over an open flame, cooked noodles and rice, all for £2 a head - and that's including a beer.

Sheds, mobile carts, stalls and roadside cafés produce exquisitely tasty food. Grilled sausages perfumed with lemongrass and mounds of fragrant sticky rice. Roasted chicken - how can it taste so good - and prawns in spicy tomato sauce.

The famous Night Markets are beautiful and crammed with people, locals and tourist parade around the streets. Lanterns give out warm golden glows and fairy lights guide the way for visitors. Perfumed, handmade soaps wrapped in delicate voile tied with tiny lengths of ribbon, intricate silver jewellery, brightly coloured hand-knitted jumpers and socks and hats, porcelain and pottery fine and fragile. Delectable smells from the many food stands waft in the air and mingle with the perfume of the flower stalls. There is no tat or nasty objects to be seen.

There are said to be over two hundred Wats (Buddhist temples) in the city. We visit the most revered and scared temple in Thailand, Wat Phra That Doi Suthep. Set on a mountain side, with the city sprawled below, it is a glorious place. On either side of the entrance sit imposing jewelled mythical sea serpents. Their ornate bodies curl themselves up the long steep staircase. Three hundred and nine steps carry the traveller to the top. A magnificent golden stupa glints in the sunlight. It's almost impossible to gaze at it. It dazzles, light bouncing off it riotously. Incense and candles burn, saffron clothed monks drift near adding to the intense peace and tranquillity of this revered space. The views are magnificent. Surrounded by lush green countryside, waterfalls appear as if by magic amongst the forests and there, down below, lies the city.

Chiang Mai caters for many 'digital nomads'. Hundreds of young people from all over the world are flocking here, many of them working. Huge numbers of cafés and offices have suddenly sprung up as a result of the arrival of all these enthusiastic youthful folks clutching their mobiles, poring over their computers. It's a gentle city and the digital nomads are a gentle creative lot; laid back, reminding me of old hippies in their cheese-cloth shirts and flowing skirts.

A follow-up visit to the hospital and Guy's good recovery means his crutches are taken away. Apparently, the first thing most surgeons ask the patient when they are carried into the hospital is,

"Scooter? Elephant? Zipwire?"

The scars from these accidents are called Farang tattoos and there are an awful lot of foreigners walking around here with them.

The surgeon is from Chiang Mai but did much of his training in Edinburgh. He has a huge affection for the Scottish city - and for Guy. He told me how impressed he was with Guy's graceful acceptance of what had happened coupled with virtually no anxiety. Makes me realise how valuable Guy's Buddhist practise is. He hasn't complained once since his leg was badly broken in many places. Do you know what, I really am in awe of him.

practice

We go to the market and buy him a smart new walking stick.

We've taken Guy and Blaire away from their room in Chiang Mai and his tombs of books. I know it's 'tomes', but tombs is a more fitting word here. Huge great things. I open one up and try with all my might to understand what is written. I get to the end of the first page and have no idea what I have just read. These are for a highly intellectual brain.

Now, he is swimming and enjoying the sunshine, but I know there's a big part of him that would rather be back in his room reading, researching, and gazing at the Buddhist temple just yards away from his window.

As I write to you there is a colossal, stone-grey, water buffalo yards from our cottage and he's looking for a puddle of water to wallow in. This being the dry season he is out of luck and now looks at me with a mixture of disdain and mild enquiry.

We are in the mountains, north of Chiang Mai. Thatched cottages set in lush gardens belong to Hamish, a dour Scot, almost a clone of Victor Meldrew - remember him? This bad-tempered, cantankerous character serves us breakfast. He is one of those people who find smiling a difficult chore. He tries but his badly fitting dentures seem to get in the way. He is not a natural host, but his partner is and makes up for Ian's lack of charm. 'Pop' is a small, very animated Thai chap who laughs at everything anyone says and everything he says. Two polar opposites who run a B&B in the back of beyond.

Blaire is a perfect companion, gentle and kind. Together we visit a Wat, a Buddhist temple. Great golden domes point up into the blue skies. Once inside, huge forty-foot commanding Buddhas look down on us. They are enigmatic, wistful and kind. Orange-robed monks everywhere, every shape and size and every age dotted around the city. Last week I found myself sitting on a cold marble floor, this was the hour and a half open meditation session. At first, it was all very serious. Older monks were sat in the front and the chanting began. Just as I was thinking I could not cope much longer with the cold of the stone floor creeping slowly but surely up my body, a flurry of young monks entered. They were quiet at first and then one by one by they started to fiddle and fidget. Lots of nose picking then a few of them started to push their neighbour, face pulling began and lots of whispering and as I watched them I quietly started to laugh. These young shaven-haired teenagers, spotty and gangling, all arms and legs inside their orange robes, were just like any other young boys. ~~delete~~

We return to Chiang Mai and tomorrow and I've got an appointment with the tailor, all a bit hit-and-miss. When they measured me for a frock, they had to get hold of a longer tape measure, I'm three times the size of a standard Thai lady.

"Madam, we will need lots of material" the tailor gleefully said.

With love,

Angie

to: family and friends

from: Joyful Traveller

subject: Austin, Texas. 2015 - Rapturous applause.

Howdy Folks,

Here we are in Austin Texas - but Austin isn't like the rest of Texas. Set right in the middle of Second Amendment, arms bearing, Stetson wearing, deeply conservative, cowboy country, Austin is an oasis. A politically liberal, laid back, socially diverse, foodie-heaven city. Huge numbers of bars, music venues and restaurants cater for every taste.

It has a reputation for having one of the best food truck cultures in the country. They reckon over 1,200 food trucks are here producing scrumptious food. I want to run from truck-to-truck eating everything on offer. Tacos bursting with exploding flavours, grilled cheese which cascades down the sides of perfectly baked sourdough toast, lobster rolls, crab cakes with heavy garlic mayonnaise and burgers that bear no resemblance to a McDonald's.

The population is exploding as more and more young people move in. Parks abound - all 300-odd of them, catering for joggers, cyclists, and walkers. There are over 30 miles of urban trails. Kayaks and swimmers fill the beautiful Lady Bird Lake. Now, the South by Southwest Film and Music Festival brings musicians, actors, performers, directors, writers, music and film enthusiasts, who take over the city. The energy is fizzing, and an air of excitement is palpable.

Kenneth has bought a tee-shirt which he's very taken with. A bright blue garment with yellow letters written boldly over the front, 'Keep Austin Weird'. And it is a bit weird and wacky here, we feel very much at home.

The scene was set when we arrived at Austin airport. There to greet us in the arrivals hall was a twelve-piece jazz band. Another band could be heard serenading departing passengers.

Austin hosts one of the biggest music and film festivals in the world, and Guy's feature-length film, Planetary, premiered here last night. I felt as though we were in a film. It was surreal and fantastic as we sat in the theatre. The excitement was almost unbearable, adrenaline wildly pumping, stomach churning, and my heart felt as if it was on fire.

Looking around the packed theatre, I realised these people had come to see the boys' film. And there they were, Steve, Christoph and Guy. I had a quiet chuckle to myself remembering how Guy and Steve would drive me crazy as rebellious, alternative, confrontational, hopelessly irresponsible schoolboys. And here they were with an air of faith and confidence, ready to show their film to a huge audience, many times over.

The film finished to rapturous applause. It's a stunningly beautiful, thought-provoking film. A question-and-answer session followed and Guy took his place on the stage. How did he know the answers to the questions that came flooding in? Complicated questions he wouldn't have had any time to prepare for. Amazing. He answered them all in a thoughtful, measured manner taking his time and making sure the questioner was satisfied.

At one point, I wanted to stand up and wildly shout,

"He's my son, look he's my son".

I didn't. I just sat there so proud, shining like a diamond. The Scotsman held my hand very tightly, trying to contain his emotions as we listened to the clapping and cheering that followed.

Afterwards, we went to a wild music bar, hung out with film and music makers - drunk on happiness.

Another showing tomorrow so more excitement to come.

With love,

Angie

to: family and friends

from: Joyful Traveller

subject: Toronto, Canada. 2015 - Toronto loves the film

Hello Everyone,

Yesterday, I sat in the biggest cinema in Toronto. Guy's film, Planetary, was being shown as part of the Toronto Environmental Film Festival.

As I arrived, I could see the crowds snaking around the corner. Hundreds of people trying to get a ticket, but it had been sold out since early that morning. The theatre was packed to the rafters and if that wasn't exciting enough, I was sitting next to an astronaut who has walked in space and notched up over a hundred and seventy-eight days on the International Space Station. He is also a charming and quite gorgeous human being.

Ron Garan features many times in Planetary and has become a great friend and business associate of Guy. They make strange bedfellows. Ron an ex-fighter pilot, crew-cut hair, a military man for a large part of his life, disciplined and a little serious - and then Guy with his flowing locks, now almost down to his waist, a Buddhist peacemaker, and a creative, exuberant soul.

On the other side of me were two of my oldest friends, Sandi and Liz.

We three met while studying for our 'O' levels, a lifetime ago. We've remained so close even after all these years. Now, here we are, the three of us, about to watch Guy's film. They both live in Canada so when I discovered the film would be shown in Toronto, they jumped at the chance to come to the Canadian premiere. I knew before I asked them that nothing would have kept them away.

Liz's husband Simon, a Welshman, along with Cerys and Rhianna, their daughters, were also there. I still haven't really forgiven

Simon. Decades ago he'd hurt me so much by whisking Lizzy off to the wilds of Canada where he started working as a doctor.

The audience applauded wildly; the clapping echoed from wall to wall. This crowd loved the film. Again, another question-and-answer session. Guy appeared even more relaxed. He could have been chatting in his kitchen over a cup of coffee instead of to over 500 people. He has now perfected his marvellous gift of making everyone in the audience think that he is talking directly to them.

After the showing, a big crowd of us trooped off to a fashionable restaurant. After heaps of delicious food and many, many bottles of wine we started the laborious task of divvying up the extremely pricey bill. We didn't need to. The Welshman had paid the whole lot. Maybe it was his way of saying sorry for taking my best friend thousands of miles away from me all those years ago.

With love,

Angie

to:	family and friends
from:	Joyful Traveller
subject:	Kuala Lumpur, Malaysia. 2016 - A return visit.

Hello Dears,

As our plane landed at Kuala Lumpur International Airport memories came flooding back, reminding me of the last time I was here. It was another lifetime ago; it was all so different then.

When I was a stewardess, I came across an extraordinary way of being able to fly around the world. Originally, the scheme had started for cabin crew who had been unwell: broken bones, infections caught overseas – any condition which meant they were not fit for the rigours of normal flying duties. A few of BA's Boeing 707s had been fitted out as freighters, cargo only, no passengers. Either a steward or stewardess was given the responsibility of looking after the three flight deck crew members consisting of a pilot, a co-pilot and a flight engineer and sometimes having to check the cargo.

Healthy crew members could volunteer for these trips, but most crew didn't. The nature of these journeys was often unpredictable – sometimes changed mid-trip - and you could never be guaranteed a return home date. It was not unusual to end up in places that didn't correspond to the original roster you were given at the start of the trip. It was a bit like a magical mystery tour and the moment I heard about this, I promptly put my name down. All you had to do was look after three flight deck crew – no demanding passengers.

Here's a gorgeous story, said to be true. A steward was disembarked in Darwin, Northern Australia, and scheduled to be picked up a few days later when a return aircraft was due to fly in from Sydney. In those days, aeroplanes didn't have the range they have today and had to refuel quite often. Darwin was basically a refuelling stop but if the weather and other conditions were right on this route, the aircraft could make it non-stop to Hong Kong or Singapore without having to refuel in Darwin. The steward had a marvellous time being stuck in Darwin, even got a part-time job at the local bar....for six whole weeks.

And here I was, a positioning B.A. crew member on my way to Kuala Lumpur. There had been some delay in Dubai, the trip had been re-routed. I had to fly to Kuala Lumpur where I would spend a couple of days on my own, eventually meeting up with another freighter and the flight crew.

I'd never been to Kuala Lumpur - it was a bit of an adventure - but sitting on that Malaysia Airlines plane I wished I'd had someone with me, that all changed.

In those days, before 9/11, some lucky passengers would be invited up to the cockpit. The Malaysia Airlines crew knew I was a positioning B.A. stewardess, and halfway through the flight I was asked if I'd like to visit the flight deck. All three crew were my age, charming and delightful. By the time the plane had touched down, the two pilots had arranged a sight-seeing tour of the city the next day. Bright and early, the two of them arrived at my hotel. Born and brought up in KL, one a Christian and the other a Hindu, I just remember two wildly exciting days. They were determined I should see everything. It became a whirlwind of visits to temples and churches, parks and museums, Chinatown and the Indian quarter, but most of all - the best street food I had ever tasted. No fancy restaurants, this was far more exciting. We ate delicious food down narrow back alleys, impossible for a tourist ever to find. There were no high-rise buildings then, no shopping malls, no upmarket coffee shops. I remember the noise - the frantic noise - the excitement; thousands of people moving around the city on bicycles, rickshaws and ancient cars. So very different now.

Back to now, and we arrived at the small hotel we'd booked. I was rummaging through a magazine rack with leaflets advertising tours, scenic adventures, and dozens of business cards from hopeful taxi drivers. An English language newspaper had been discreetly placed at the back of the rack in the hope, presumably, that no tourist would find it. It reported that the city was on 'High Alert' after a potential suicide bomber had been planning to detonate a device in one of the shopping centres. Also, an attempt to kidnap the Prime Minister had recently been foiled. Kenneth said,

"Well, that's handy, it'll keep the crowds away", and it did.

We have been roaming around the city, at times, it's eerily quiet. Glittering skyscrapers compete with quaint old coffee shops and chophouses. Elegant, sophisticated restaurants sit alongside tumble-down food shacks and hawkers' carts so old they creak raucously when in motion. The gigantic shopping malls were still crammed with people, but an atmosphere of fear and watchfulness permeated the place.

We walked alone around the charming Merdeka Square. This is where the Union Jack was lowered, and the Malaysian flag was hoisted high into the air in August 1957 when independence was declared.

Kenneth was keen to visit the Petronas Twin Towers, the highest twin towers in the world. Rising up from the ground, towers glistening, steel wrapped. They dominate the skyline, futuristic and strange and, I thought, a prime target for bombers. So, we just wondered around the base of them feeling a bit sad with the world as it is.   wandered

All that changed when we found the Old China Café. A place Guy had insisted we visit, it was one of his favourites, and he was right. Amazing what a huge plate of delicious food can do for the soul. On the outskirts of Chinatown along a row of grubby, dilapidated pre–World War 1 shophouses. Shophouses are buildings with shopfronts at the front and rooms for owners to live in at the back. They are now tumbling down, developers itching to get their greedy, grubby hands on them.

Battered old wooden doors swung inwards at the entrance to the Old China Café and there in front of us was a delirious mixture of old black and white photographs covering most of the wall. Peeling wallpaper, old marble-topped tables and randomly placed fridges - so old some leaned dangerously to one side. Assorted bunches of flowers seemed to appear out of the gloom cast by the ancient wood. It all added to a feeling that we might have stumbled into a film set.

The food was scrumptious, still not quite sure what we were throwing down our throats. The waiter seemed to think he knew best, so we left it to him. There was a slimy looking thing that had the appearance of an eyeball. I gallantly closed my eyes and took a bite; it was quite delicious and then I consumed the whole plump concoction. The only time I've ever had food poisoning was in a posh hotel in Nairobi. The meal was ten times the price I would usually pay and I ended up seriously sick.

Penang tomorrow. The host of the Airbnb insists on meeting us from the bus stop, not quite sure why as his place only looks a few yards away. Interesting, as his emails have been a bit disjointed, it might be a language barrier though. More soon.

With love,

Angie

to: family and friends

from: Joyful Traveller

subject: Penang, Malaysia - Flashpackers

Penang, often referred to as The Pearl of the Orient and fondly regarded as the food capital of Malaysia. It's a melting pot of Chinese, Malay and Indian cultures that, amazingly, seem to happily co-exist together, most of the time. Churches, mosques, Chinese and Hindu temples sit next to each other.

It's only 8 miles wide and 16 miles long but so much is packed into it, you could be mistaken for thinking it's ten times the size. Stunningly gorgeous white sand beaches skirt the island, while inland is an uninhabitable jungle.

It was one of the first places to be colonised by the British. Penang became an important port, hence the island is flooded with colonial style architecture. Some preserved, some magnificently decaying adding to the intriguing mood of the island. The old part of Georgetown, the capital, remains a maze of bustling streets, full of life – much like it would have been a century ago.

There is a sense here of preserving the old way of life, many inhabitants are from an older generation. Age-old coffee shops still abound and there are hawkers' carts everywhere. Ancient old contraptions, free standing with huge wheels, selling moveable feasts.

Chinese families whose forebears have been here since the ninetieth century still occupy wooden homes built on the jetties. Here, life seems to have stood still. Timbered boardwalks lead onto rickety wooden homes, the sea gently lapping at the stilts which, miraculously, seem to hold them up. We walked amongst fishermen repairing their nets while small children played in the narrow walkways. There was the sound of cooking pots rattling and delicious smells emanating from every home.

The food is scrumptious. They say the roadside vendors serve some of the best takeaway food in the world. Noodles come in all shapes and sizes; rice noodles, wheat noodles, egg noodles, clear vermicelli ones as thin and as light as air, great fat ones resembling doughnuts. All accompanied by a vast variety of sauces, hot spicy ones, mild fragrant ones. Laksa is the name of a particular type of noodle soup and my favourite is the curried coconut one. It is so easy to eat. I can shovel it into my mouth in record time now.

The markets are bursting with rip-off designer stuff: handbags, watches, jewellery, clothes, trainers, jackets - anything that a so-called 'designer' stamp or logo can be plonked on. Piled high on moveable trollies. Vendors shouting after each prospective customer, claiming everything to be 'genuine'.

The Scotsman is exceedingly happy as we only have two small suitcases and no room even for a handkerchief. That gives me an idea. I might just write a little article entitled, 'How to travel around Asia for six weeks with a very small suitcase'.

We reached Penang after a comfortable four-hour train ride from Kuala Lumpur followed by an extremely unpleasant ferry trip. It was only a half-hour jaunt in a gigantic iron, rust encased vessel with a rattling that shook our bones and a rumbling that's still ringing in my ears.

Getting off the bus in Georgetown, we were greeted by a teenager,

"Aw, my first Flash-Packers I meet", he said with much excitement.

We are now official 'Flash-Packers' (no back-pack, just two small nifty suitcases on wheels).

Angry notices, six foot high, greet us in the hallway into the apartments.

NO AIRBNB HERE. IT IS AGAINST MANAGEMENT RULES TO ALLOW PAID GUESTS.

We stare at the notices as he takes us aside,

"You be part of my family from now on, okay?".

I don't like to tell him that that would appear highly unlikely, but we smile watching his concerned face.

The apartment turns out to have one bedroom. The teenager cheerfully tells us that while we are staying, he will sleep on the sofa bed.

I am in need of a good hot shower. I take the little hand towel - the only one on the bed and stand under the shower. I then realise there is no shower curtain or bathmat. Slippery tiles are lethal, so I desperately try to stop water from going all over the floor. I carefully tiptoe into the bedroom and do a bit of searching. One lone pillow on the double bed, curtains that refuse to close, no bedside lamp and not an inch of space in the small wardrobe.

The kitchen which he had marketed as 'fully equipped' came with a couple of plates, a bit of cutlery and one small saucepan.

He was such a dear boy. An eighteen-year-old in his first year of university, earnest and caring but he'd managed to spend all his student loan. He spoke of his parents, authoritarian and disciplined, they could not be told of his financial problems.

The next day we went shopping. We worked out that with the money we were paying him he could buy another pillow, a shower curtain, a bathmat and a towel. We made a plan. There were other guests arriving after us. We, he confided, were his very first guests.

The next shopping trip would be for a couple of lamps and some coat hangers and maybe, I suggested,

"You might be better off describing the kitchen facilities as, 'basic' until you buy more utensils".

He was so happy with this arrangement, we then took him out for supper and Kenneth fixed the curtain tracking.

Tomorrow we go on to Langkawi, another island - close to the Thai border. Our young man looked a little concerned when we told him we'd be taking the ferry. When questioning him in more detail, he tried gallantly to brush off any concerns he might have,

"Oh, you are very well travellers, I wouldn't worry…much"

Um, I'll let you know exactly what he meant next time.

With love,

Angie

to: family and friends

from: Joyful Traveller

subject: Langkawi, Malaysia. It's true, life does flash before your eyes when you think you're a gonner.

Dearest Ones,

I now understand the alarmed look on our host's face; he didn't want to reveal the horror of the ferry crossing.

I've just looked at TripAdvisor comments for the first time, just to check I wasn't being too much of a wimp. The headings range from, 'I thought it was my last" to 'the most terrible journey of my life' and, 'I became a believer and kissed the ground thanking God I was still alive'.

Ready for this?

I breathed a sigh of relief on seeing the boat. A little battered around the edges but nothing too shocking, almost up-market from the last one we sailed on.

I suppose it might have been a bad omen when the crew hurriedly started handing out sick bags before we had departed. But no, I settled into my seat trying not to be too churlish as more and more passengers arrived and squeezed into our row, forcing us to keep our arms flat against our bodies.

The surly crew had piled luggage up against the windows and now it was stacked so high there was little daylight shining through, impossible to see out. I decided I would relax and go with the flow. The boat jerked into action and we were away. I tried to crane my neck, the only part of my body I could move now, as bags from my fellow passengers were sliding onto my legs pinning them together. Most of the passengers were Malaysian with worried looks on their faces: looks I've seen hundreds of times on aeroplanes. It's a combination of terror and foreboding. I started to feel a little disturbed.

The open waters between these two islands are notoriously rough and today they were at their most demented. The boat started heaving and as it did half the passengers followed suit. The heady aroma of vomit and diesel fumes became overpowering.

The Scotsman, who prides himself on being an experienced sailor, started to look green around the gills. I heaved my breakfast up and then some more along with the lady who sat next to me. We had no language in common apart from the sick that was bonding us in some strange and rather special way. She handed me a tissue and a mint and demonstrated how I had to suck it very slowly. I did as she recommended and then threw that up too. Another sweetie along with more tissues were offered.

By now there seemed to be quite a bit of praying going on. Some crossing of chests by a few terrified tourists, prayer beads and a bit of howling and lots of wailing thrown into the mix.

Kenneth escaped to get "some air" and reappeared about two minutes later. I cannot do justice to how he looked; wind-blown doesn't do it, he had been in a hurricane and soaked to the skin.

"You can't go to the toilet, it's outside, impossible to get to and full of sea water. Besides, I had to climb over a mountain of suitcases and now they've all slid over and are blocking the entrance".

We were in a coffin, a sealed one, impossible to escape from. They played a video of The Planet of the Apes and then repeated it. I think apes might feature in my nightmares to come.

We eventually managed to escape from the death trap, most of us sick and covered in sweat. I now understood why the crew were so unpleasant and felt quite sorry for them. I forgot to mention that in the middle of the voyage the engineer emerged from the front cabin, where the lunatic captain was hurtling his boat at the elements, and he promptly threw up - missing his sick bag - and depositing the contents of his stomach onto the floor of the boat. I wondered if he did this on every crossing.

Arriving at our guest house deep into the undergrowth were a collection of dear little blue painted stone huts, surrounding a covered courtyard. A collection of colourful rattan chairs and sofas for guests to mingle, bohemian and stylish.

A rather gorgeous looking chap dressed in fine linen was there to greet us. I apologised for our appearance and odour. He seemed completely unfazed, probably most of his guests arrive in the same state.

"Is the fish and chip shop still there in Princess Victoria Street?"

I was still a bit disorientated and now, thousands of miles away from home, on a small island standing in a Malaysian jungle we were being asked this question. It turns out he had been a student at Bristol University and lodged above our local chippie.

Tomorrow a friend of his was visiting and I was told I must be sure to meet him. The next day his friend did appear - and I knew his face. It turns out his mother lives just along the road from us and he visits her regularly!

There's a big fat frog that lurks around our toilet seat.

Kenneth says he's welcome, he will eat the mossies and other creepy crawlies. I have to investigate thoroughly before I use the loo, and so this is a little ritual I now have to incorporate into my daily routine. Must go now and see if he's made an appearance.

I've got a stick to gently coax him out. Sometimes he just looks at me, a bit like a defiant teenager not wanting to get out of bed in the morning.

With love,

Angie

to: family and friends

from: Joyful Traveller

subject: Somewhere on the coast of Malaysia - Fascinating
           encounter

Hello Lovely Ones,

There was something definitely not quite right. It started off
when I went to book this bed and breakfast. Lots of furtiveness,
odd messages backwards and forwards. Alexei with a strong
eastern European accent wanted to know an awful lot about
our trip. Why we were in Malaysia? Exactly what we were doing
here? A bit of an inquisition took place. I could have forgotten
the whole thing, but I became quite intrigued and was so glad I
persevered.

We arrived to find Alexei and his partner Renat waiting on the
doorstep, (for their safety, I'll tell you all about that in a minute,
I have changed their names) They must have been standing at
their window looking out for us.

There was a feeling of anxiousness as though something was
wrong. For two days they were helpful and generous and deeply
controlling. The use of the kitchen was part of the booking.

We bought fresh fish. We watched as the boats arrived.
Fishermen's faces the colour of caramelised toffee throwing fish
to customers on the jetty. I shouted like a local and caught two
perfect fish as they whizzed by my head, no idea what they were.
We threw money at the boat and left, carrying our supper home
in some dubious old newspaper.

Returning to the apartment, there they were, lying in wait, the
odd couple. I showed them the fish. Alexei, the cook, looked
alarmed. I haven't mentioned the state of the apartment -
how perfectly spotless everything was. Nothing out of place,
gleaming surfaces, floors you really could eat your dinner off.
Every time we used the bathroom Renat would rush in and flick

a cloth around, no escaped drips or soap suds allowed. This behaviour I realised, was a way of controlling a part of their lives which they could have some control over, as opposed to the rest of it that they could not.

Alexei grabbed the fish and announced that he would be cooking. Me in the kitchen, messing up his perfection of a place, was too much for him to contemplate. He cooked the fish to perfection and started to look happy. That was day two.

By day three I think they had either had enough of my endless questions and had to give in, or they genuinely wanted to talk. I hope the latter was true. I felt at times like a terrier with a bone, they fascinated me. What were two, gay, eastern European men doing in Malaysia looking like frightened rabbits, particularly strange for a forty-odd-year-old man with biceps the size of small mountains?

It's a crazy story and that's why I love all this travelling. People are endlessly fascinating, complicated and amazing.

Alexei had been a train driver. He had witnessed many, many, horrifying suicides on the tracks in front of his train. With no training on how to cope with these events, and no form of counselling after the events, he was left damaged, bruised and broken.

Renat had been a bodyguard. Who his boss was, was a secret, shrouded in mystery - but he had been some big-shot. Just when I was starting to think this all can't be real, Renat lifted his trouser leg and there I saw a mottled, horrible, purple-coloured hole. A gunshot wound right in the middle of his left shin.

That evening, their story unfolded as we sat together eating a delicious eastern European goulash they had insisted on cooking for us. Their story was about escape and a need to find a safe place in the world. Where they came from, homosexuality was despised and reviled but that wasn't the problem now. The only source of income they had was their B&B and they were super vigilant, almost paranoid, about who their guests were. Was Renat maybe fearing some sort of reprisal, another shot in the leg – or worse? He muttered many times about certain men and how they couldn't be trusted. Alexei, too, had, apparently, quit his train driver job under something of a cloud. I was sure there was more but by then I was exhausted and so terribly plastered.

The vodka bottles were finished - and so was I. We said goodnight and then there were lots of hugs and smiles and an air of lightness and relief surrounded them which had not been there before.

We had to leave very early the next morning. There was no sign of our hosts. The apartment was pristine, as usual. The numerous empty vodka bottles had all vanished and the table had been carefully set. Delicious pastries, croissants and some strange looking sliced meats were carefully arranged and then there, in the middle of the table, was a note that simply said, 'Thank you', with two large kisses.

With love,

Angie

Hello Everyone,

Here we are in Singapore, of course we weren't meant to be in Singapore. We optimistically thought we'd be safely tucked up at home by now, eating Heinz baked beans on a nice softly toasted slice of wholemeal bread.

I'm often asked about stand-by and the unfathomable workings behind it. Now seems a good opportunity to explain, but before I witter on, I need to tell you this. I have never taken it for granted, never. I have always felt unbelievably lucky and if I do a bit of moaning well, it's pleasurable moaning.

We ended up in Hong Kong having looked at "the loads". That is the magical number of possible empty seats available, and airline crew have access to this vital piece of information. Hong Kong looked good, Singapore not so. We arrived bright and breezy and reported to the standby desk.

Stand-by is a case of feast or famine, mostly feast, we usually end up in Business or if we are very lucky, First Class. In First Class you adopt a mask, celebrities merge into the bulkheads, everyone with an air of entitlement and playing it all so cool. I try not to look too excited when the food arrives, delicious, scrumptious food served at 35,000 feet. Pyjamas are offered, the seat is slowly lowered and if by magic, turned into a sumptuous relaxing bed complete with a snug duvet and pillows as soft as marshmallows.

Depending on where you are in the world, stand-by desks can range from whole rooms with fancy screens and tannoy systems, to tiny half abandoned back-rooms miles away from the departure gates.

It is organised on seniority, on how important you are deemed to be in the company's pecking order. The higher up the ladder you are, the higher up the standby list you appear.

"This flight is overbooked". These are the dreaded words no standby passenger wants to hear, "Please stand to the right, listen out for your name". So, we stood, and we stood, and we stood, all the while eyeing up the other standbys.

We often play a game, watching them closely deciding where they might fit into the company. They might be important heads of departments, baggage handlers, training captains, directors, check-in staff, or toilet cleaners.

Pilots and their wives are easy to spot: short hair with boring sports jackets - safe skirts and sensible shoes for the wives (except for my friend Judith, who is nothing at all like that)

Cabin crew, I can spot them a mile away, my tribe. A little flamboyant, colourful, the stewards fiercely groomed, knowing what the score is. The stewardesses clutching extremely well made often fake, designer handbags, sunglasses permanently on top of their head whatever the weather and lipstick, always lipstick. To this day, I can't leave the house without my lipstick on.

This time, no name was called and the scramble to 'wait list' for the next flight was intense, possibly no seat home for several days.

We hopped on a flight to Singapore. Bad move.

The area around the stand-by desk was littered with passengers in various stages of despair. Singapore Airlines flight had gone 'US' (some bit of the aircraft wasn't performing as it should do). Fare-paying passengers were being transferred to our BA flights, two flights that night, all chock-a-block now.

"Please could all standby passengers return tomorrow night by 6pm, goodnight".

We made a dash for the hotel booking desk knowing rooms would be heavily discounted; it was after midnight. We did this for three nights and became quite acquainted with all the various airport staff, including the driver of the courtesy bus to and from the hotel. The first night he welcomed us on board and smiled broadly. The second night his smile was not so broad, and he took on a quizzical air. By the third night he had stopped smiling. Why did this crazy couple go off to the airport every night only to return again heaving heavy suitcases with downcast faces?

Fourth day and I started to feel a little panicky. Will the rest of our life be spent shuttling between Singapore airport and a cheap hotel - like a part in a horror film, never able to escape? I then remember all the standby flights we have taken, racing around the world, Guy and Nessie trailing after us.

You can never be sure of getting to your desired destination if you have a transit stop. On one occasion the Scotsman and I had agreed if anyone was going to be 'off-loaded' (politely asked to leave the aircraft) then Kenneth would go with Guy. We were coming back from the Seychelles via Nairobi. I didn't want to be left in Nairobi on my own or with Ness. With a look of pain and concern the stewardess made her way down the aisle stopping in front of us. We knew. It's that look that says she's terribly sorry but two people had to scarper. The boys ended up having a bit of an African safari adventure, a fabulous couple of days together.

Staff Travel teaches you never to rely on any travel plans - actually, don't make plans.

One another occasion our lovely and helpful check-in lady announced as we all stood expectantly around her desk (I always frantically cross my fingers behind my back, willing seats to magically appear)

"Flight to San Diego is overbooked but I can put you four on the flight to Phoenix if that's any good?" Kenneth sent me off to the airport WH Smith's,

"Have a look at a map and find out how far Phoenix is from San Diego".

I pored over a map and returned indicating with my thumb and forefinger the measurement of an inch, but I'd forgotten to find out how many miles an inch represented. In the end, the Arizona desert and the long drive to California was fabulous.

Nessie, as a small child, once sat in the cockpit on the way home from Rome (before 9/11) inches away from the back of the captain's head. I told him she had a habit of throwing up. He laughed and said, "I've got six back home, what's a bit of sick"?

It's a tense situation on take-off and I knew this five-year-old must not make a sound. To this day I am full of shame. I had to do something nastily underhand. Our treasured Border Collie, Dixie, was waiting for us at the kennels back home. Each time Nessie looked as though she was going to say something I whispered "Dixie" reminding her that if she said a word we wouldn't go and pick up her beloved dog. She didn't talk or throw up that time.

Back to the Singapore standby queue. You can spot the new standbys, all eager to make use of the drinks trolley after take-off, maybe wondering what film they might decide to watch, alerting loved ones to their ETA (estimated time of arrival)

We stand there hardly daring to breath as the list of names is called out. Ours, yes ours, can it be? Are we going to get a seat and be on our way home? Oh joy, Oh Staff Travel I will never, ever complain again. We almost skip to the desk. Yes, here we are all ready to run to the gate. By the way if you ever see passengers frantically running as though their life depended on it, then often it's a standby one. Running through vast corridors, running through security, running to the gates which are just about to close.

"Jump seats OK? - quickly now, the flight is departing very soon".

By now, if they had told us we'd be attached to the outside wing to get home I would have agreed.

"Jump seat". A jump seat is the size of a large postage stamp. It's that tiny little pull-down seat at the far end of an aeroplane which sits right next door to the lavatories. Only crew or ex-crew are allowed to place their bottoms on it. Ours were going to be on it for over fourteen hours. The seat is so small, unless you use the large harness that clamps you in, you would roll out of it. The seat is vertical with no head rest, so you sit bolt upright for the duration of the journey. The air conditioning on a 747 works by violently ending up flowing under the emergency chute which happens to be right by any leg room you might have.

The crew look with a mixture of pity and concern as you take your place. They will do anything to make your flight bearable. So it was that the Scotsman and I, either side of the lavatories, found ourselves wrapped in first class blankets with bottles of champagne for company.

Aircraft toilet doors are not all the same design; some you have to push, some you pull. In the middle of the night sleepy passengers often are found wrestling with the problem and I would come to their rescue acting as a sort of toilet monitor. Other passengers looked at me with a mixture of surprise and incredulity. One asked how long I had been a toilet attendant and did I like my job; some kind soul proffered a tip! Several passengers were so concerned they offered me their own seat for a little while.

Sat upright for seventeen hours (there was a long delay on the ground that night) freezing cold, assuming the role of a toilet monitor is a bit of a test. If I ever do fly like a 'normal' person again I'd be bound to miss the drama of it all. Getting on a flight and knowing I would be guaranteed a seat, um...not much adventure in that.

With love,

Angie

to: family and friends

from: Joyful Traveller

subject: Missouri, U.S.A. 2016 - Gun and ticks amongst breath taking skies.

Hello Everyone,

Locals often pronounce their state as, 'Misery' not least when referring to the weather. Two extremes; summer - hot and sticky, winter - fierce and freezing. Coupled with tornados and the odd hurricane.

Before we left home, I did a bit of research. A solid Republican state and home to some of the most obese people in America - all within the 'Bible Belt'. Here, evangelical, fundamentalist Christians rule the roost.

One comment on a page entitled, 'Why should you live in Missouri?', stood out.

"It has the most restrictive laws on abortion, marijuana and public government access but on the flip side it has some of the least restrictive laws on property and firearms ownership and sex offenses".

Someone had written underneath, "Great if you're a wealthy, gun-toting paedophile".

We were in for and interesting month. Oh, and 11 million turkeys are slaughtered here every year.

We are looking after a collection of dogs, chickens and a few ducks. It turned out, the dogs had not been given any anti-tick treatment or medication. This all changed with a frantic call to the owners after I had read extensively about Lyme disease. Instead of the nasty, wriggling little blighters infesting the dogs' coats, they now lie dead at our feet.

After our twice-daily walks, The Scotsman and I have to take off all our clothes, stand naked and make a scrupulous inspection of each other. Not the most romantic of pastimes. Yesterday, Kenneth found two of them making their way up my back even though every part of my body had been covered with clothes. They can wriggle their way in through the tiniest of openings.

Ticks seem to run my life here, I'm always on the alert.

The nearest neighbours are a few miles up a dirt road. A father and son. The son definitely has foetal alcohol syndrome. They knocked on the door the other day, the son unable to take his eyes off my chest which was, unfortunately, encased in a tight strap top.

They stood on the doorstep and assured us they were allowed to borrow farming equipment stuff. Naively, we believed them. They were neighbours, after all and don't farming folk help each other out?

"They knows us, you hand it over". Their pick-up truck had a collection of rifles visible in the back.

After an awkward telephone call with the owners a few days later, we were instructed to go and retrieve the farm machine immediately.

Deliverance, the movie, has always stayed with me and here we were outside a home that could have jumped off the film set. A low building the windows of which were taped with rotting newspaper. Some of the windowsills had disintegrated so badly that great planks of soiled wood had been nailed to the connecting walls. The front door held no paint, only dirt and grime where countless filthy hands had pushed it open. In the yard, not a blade of grass in sight, stubby bits of parched earth held a huge assortment of - it's hard to describe - an assortment of discarded objects, broken and useless: old farm implements and machinery, half dismantled washing machines, bits of suspicious-looking metal, six or seven abandoned vehicles. The vehicle windows were long gone and now only glimpses of greenery trailed from the roof: hardy, indestructible plants had taken root amongst the chaos of the interior.

At the far end of the yard, I spied a vast array of beer cans that appeared to have fallen haphazardly into the dirt. On top of the wall, more cans sat patiently waiting to be shot. So, this was where the nightly sound of gunfire came from. The sound would puncture the evening air making us feel rather vulnerable and a bit jittery.

"We need to collect the machine you borrowed, your neighbours need it returned now", Kenneth said in his calm voice with an edge of authority.

The father and son looked particularly annoyed. I got the impression they were weighing up whether it was worth a fight, but grudgingly decided against it. They pointed to the wretched machine leaving Kenneth and I to manoeuvre it into the truck. I noticed he drove home at a much faster speed that normal and checked, twice that the doors were locked that night.

Missouri has some of the most liberal gun laws in America. Everyone seems to have the right to own a gun and many of them have several. Our two neighbours with their guns were a worry. On the local news one evening there was a report about a particularly gruesome gun fight in St Louis. When interviewed, a local resident declared,

"I love living here. Sure, there are consequences but no place is perfect. The crime is bad but get yourself a big, angry dog and a gun and you'll be fine".

A local fair was taking place and we decided to visit. It was a family affair, tons of children running around and lots of guns. A notice informed visitors: 'no concealed weapons permitted'. There were fathers with children, holding their little hands, watching them laughing on the roundabouts, aiming balls at coconut shies, eating huge long hotdogs while carrying them on their shoulders and all the while big, bulging guns sticking out of their pockets, for all to see.

This is Trump country. "The Word Became Flesh, John I.14" with a picture alongside it of the person that many people hoped would be the next president of the United States. This was on a huge billboard and although pressure mounted to have it taken down there was a lot of opposition. It seemed that every lawn had Trump for President placards proudly on display.

Along with the Trump advertising were anti-abortionist billboards. I couldn't make my mind up which I loathed more. Pictures of beautiful bouncing babies alongside messages like this 6ft one we passed on a highway: 'In God's court abortion is MURDER' A local community church had put this one up. A few miles down the road another one:

'Thanks Mom, for choosing LIFE', with another picture of a beautiful baby plastered above the message.

The dogs are a joy to look after, each with its own distinctive personality. The great outdoors goes on forever, rich yellow fields of corn under a huge blue sky. There is no light pollution here so at night we can see stars we never knew existed twinkling in a vast, expansive sky. Missouri's beauty is in Nature; here in all its glory, surroundings us, permeating us with its very spirit.

I can play loud, loud music and dance on the grass and our adopted duckling follows me everywhere. She was born the day the owners left and she has imprinted herself on Kenneth and I. That's what ducks do, we learnt; the first thing they see becomes their parent. We are so ridiculous and treat her as though she is a child, one of ours. Kenneth has made her a cage, somewhere safe at night. In the day she is with us constantly, even the dogs who have been brought up with ducks know not to get to too close to her. She has us wrapped around her fluffy little feet. She sits and watches television with us and insists on sitting on the keyboard as I type this. I worry what will become of her when we leave, I fear the other ducks will not accept her.

Kenneth went off for supplies and stopped off at a local bar. He was intrigued by the large number of sit-on lawnmowers in the car park. People here are a little suspicious of strangers and we stick out like a sore thumb - but they are also friendly. The barman started chatting to Kenneth and Kenneth asked him if there was a lawnmower conference going on. The barman roared with laughter,

"That's there is sure no conference; that's there all those dudes what's been done for drunk driving"

Apparently, you can't get arrested for being over the limit on a sit-on lawnmower. As he left, Kenneth spied an old chap speeding away from the bar on his F1 lawnmower.

I must go now; the dogs need a walk. It takes quite a time to dress myself to make sure those evil little ticks don't make a meal of me.

With love,

Angie

to: family and friends

from: Joyful Traveller

subject: London....a week later

There I was, passing St Pancras station, admiring the architecture, watching all the commuters scurrying by, hugely enjoying the scene. My dearest friend Chrissie is driving.

I'd just delivered a two-day Presentation Skills course to an enthusiastic audience. I'm sitting back, relaxing, and go to push my hair out of my face. My hand lands on something round and hard on the crown of my head and in that moment, I panic and pull frantically at the thing. A fat, engorged tick wriggles in my hand. Blood spurts out as I attempt to squash it.

We arrive back at Chrissie's home and she peers at the tick site on my head. I am sure there is still something embedded in my head, it doesn't feel right.

"No", Chrissie says empathically, looking through her less than perfect spectacles, "Nothing there".

I have the foresight to keep it, horrid little thing, wrapped-up in an empty crisp packet I just happened to have in my handbag. Jean, my marvellous medical friend, a knowledgeable and highly competent doctor, who I often turn to in a health crisis (as you can imagine, this happens quite frequently and I am always met with much kindness mixed with practicality - just what a hypochondriac needs) told me, when I had called from Missouri in a frenzy concerning ticks and Lyme disease, this is what I had to do. Keep the little blighter and if I develop signs within ten days then it can be tested for Lyme disease.

Of course, being a chronic hypochondriac I started to suffer a number of odd symptoms that night.

Nessie met me at Temple Meads train station in Bristol and there, on the platform, I insisted she examine my head.

"Oh, Ma, I can see at least two things sticking up, they look like little legs".

I bolted to the health centre and, unbelievably, was seen by a South African nurse who liked nothing better than to extract ticks,

"Do you know what? I've missed these little buggers", she chuckled.

Ten days have passed and I'm still upright. I tell Chrissie she needs new glasses. I keep the horrid tick, just in case .... you never know.

With love,

Angie

to: family and friends

from: Joyful Traveller

subject: Nusa Lembongan 2017: small island off the coast
of Bali. Sometimes you get it wrong

Hi Lovely Ones,

Kenneth and I all neat and tidy, our chic suitcases by our sides as we stood on the shore, waiting for our boat to arrive. We've been staying in Sanur, a laid back very respectable town, lots of older ex-pats and great coffee and croissants each day but fancied a bit of an adventure. We were off to an island beloved by surfers. Cut-off shorts, flip flops, backpacks and sun-kissed young skin surrounded us. How pleasingly they looked as they leapt on to the boat, moored a few yards off the beach.

Kenneth rolled up his trousers, gallantly taking my large handbag along with his suitcase and backpack. I struggled desperately trying to hold my suitcase above the water, hitching my dress above my waist, now all was exposed. We flung our cases over the side and clambered aboard, hot and sweaty - and wet.

The boat was an ancient wooden affair that creaked and heaved over the waves taking my stomach with it. The indignity of showing my knickers and rounded bottom as well as our antics trying to clamber into the boat, was topped off with me throwing-up, very near these relaxed, arthritic-free young ones. I stared hard at the tiny island we were heading for and breathed deeply.

The heavens opened and with no cover to the boat, water started sloshing around our feet. Alarmed, I glanced at The Scotsman who was enjoying it all hugely. The boat limped towards the island, rough waves surrounding us, when a deeply handsome blue-eyed boy stood up, grabbed my suitcase saying in a strong Australian accent,

"Don't worry Doll, I'll carry it ashore for you".

I didn't care then that I was soaked, bruised and battered or that I felt extremely seasick. I had been called, a 'Doll'. All was well.

Most times we get it right - usually spot on - and very occasionally we get it completely wrong. This time it was a complete disaster. I wanted to get exceedingly irate with Airbnb, but this proved impossible to do and was deeply frustrating.

It started off with the driver of the pickup truck. These strange trucks have small engines and worn-out wooden bench seats that rocket you around from side to side. This is the only form of transport on this tiny island apart from the dreaded scooters. He stopped at the end of an unmade track and refused to take us to the door of the guest house even though sheets of rain were still descending like waterfalls,

"No Madam, far too, too many holes for my liking", said as he deposited us at the end of the narrow, uninviting alley.

I understood what he meant as we navigated the potholes. They had been filling up for most of the day and now a substantial deluge was threatening to submerge the alley. Torrential rain fell, mixing the mud with various other bits of suspicious looking debris. The holes got deeper the further we tottered trying to manoeuvre our suitcases with wheels that now refused to turn as the mud strangled them. Filth ran up our trouser legs and clothes stuck tight to our bodies.

A shabby sign announced our arrival, directing us to an unloved courtyard. A laid-back collection of beautiful creatures looking like how you might imagine professional surfers to be, were lazing around worn-out sofas and lazy chairs. They were shielded from the rains by huge canopies formed out of old greying palms and bits of bamboo. There was an air of decay mixed with a strong smell of dope and Kenneth and I stood there looking …..ridiculous.

A rickety old sign informed new arrivals that this was, 'Reception'. Sprawled over the counter was a young woman. Clad in a bikini top consisting of a few strategically placed bits of string that allowed her abundant array of tattoos to career wildly around her body. We both stood and gawped. My pearls still in place, my linen dress sagging around my body, now sticking to all the wrong places. Kenneth's white linen trousers were a shade of poo and his expensive Panama hat was creased and battered, matching his face at that point.

She enquired several times if we had arrived at our correct destination even though there in front of her was our reservation. I wondered, did she think there might be a younger, cooler, hippier couple arriving that day with the same surname? Reluctantly, she handed over the key and immediately resumed her same stance occupying more of the counter. When I turned to look back, she was sound asleep.

The room smelt rotten, musty and damp but there was a mosquito net; the most important, the most vital piece of equipment for anywhere in the rural Far East. It was folded neatly at each corner of the bed and tied with a piece of fraying string. We decided we needed to be more chilled and not so spoilt.

The shower was down some steps in a sort of basement arrangement which was open to the elements. You had to hang on very tightly to the handrail as the steps were broken and deadly uneven in many places. One sharp tug of the handrail would have probably wrenched it clean away taking half the wall with it. Sludgy looking pools of water coagulated around the lone shower outlet. Wanting to wash the mud, sweat and grime that had accumulated on my skin I turned the taps on. No hot water, just a measly trickle of tepid, yellow-coloured liquid. Kenneth looked at the geyser concluding that the thermostat wasn't working. I still smelt a little like our room did when I went looking for the manager.

He was friendly and smiley, until I explained we had no hot water. His face then became blank,

"I don't know much about the place".

He was a surfer from Australia called Dale, had sort of stepped in as relief manager to earn some cash while the owner was away.

"Where did he go?"

"Don't know, great mystery, but he checks in every week...or two".

"We need hot water".

"I don't know much about hot water either".

We sat at the bar and I got sloshed on some suspicious looking cocktails.

Smelly, and secretly wishing I was somewhere else we clambered into bed and unfurled the mosquito net. Looking up at the ceiling I realised, after a while, I could see big patches of it, the net was broken in many places. Drink and fear took over. I threw on a few clothes and scurried back to the bar. Dale was there. I interrupted his dreaming and pleaded with him to give us an undamaged mosquito net.

"I don't know much about mosquito nets".

My first impulse was to shake him horribly hard but realised it wouldn't make a scrap of difference, he probably didn't know much about hysterical women either.

Being prepared travellers, we carry our 'emergency pack' - full of all sorts of useful objects. Large plastic clothes pegs were extracted. I almost broke my neck balancing on top of the bed, my head swirling with alcohol and rage. I swayed horribly while handing the pegs to Kenneth who ineptly tried to cover the offending holes. I enraged the Scotsman by spraying copious amounts of a 'Deet'-based anti-mossie product (possibly toxic - but it's the only stuff that works) on to him and the bedclothes.

Shall I tell you why I reacted in this way? You might be thinking that it's all down to my neurosis or obsessive personality, but that would not be quite fair. We had been warned that Dengue fever was rife at the moment, especially on the islands. We would be ok. Lots of foul 'Deet' protector, frequent hot showers. The Dengue mosquito, Aedes, just loves sweat and dirt and, unlike other types of mosquito, is active during the day. So, nothing much to worry about....

Dengue fever is not a great disease to catch the first time around but if caught a second time it becomes deadlier and, with slightly older people can be life threatening.

It thrives in dirty, dark, damp places. Looking under the bed there was a fine, neat pile of human dirt and hair, bits of cigarette papers, an old toothpaste tube and weeks of dust - a very appealing home for the dreaded Dengue insect. A mosquito net with gaping holes coupled with two stinky, well covered, as in lots of tasty flesh and fat to nip at; we were a delicious dinner just waiting to be devoured.

It's interesting how the human bladder reacts when put into a stressful situation. Normally, I might need to pee once a night and sometimes not at all. That night, I wanted to pee every half an hour. The dash to the lavatory involved running around the bed and careering down eight wobbly steps to a tiny room with an open, glassless window. By now, I could hardly see as the vile 'Deet' had morphed into my eyes and my silk nightie was no defence against the Dengue flying monsters. Clambering back into bed I scratched and scratched, convinced they had got me. The Scotsman, meanwhile, slept on and on, totally oblivious to my night of hell.

Calling Airbnb in the morning was not a pleasant experience, fraught and frustrating. It seems they prefer the client and the owners to, 'sort out situations amongst themselves and try to come to some sort of amicable arrangement'.

They give you three or four days to do this. I tried to explain I would probably be hospitalised by then, or even worse, if we stayed in this dirty, crummy place. Dale meanwhile, kept running off the minute he caught sight of me. I tried to leg it after him once but he was too quick for me.

It has ended up with a few rude emails between the owner and me and, at the moment, only a refund for a couple of nights - we had booked for a week.

I have to go now, feeling a little fraught as we can't stay here any longer and there doesn't seem to be any available places to stay on this tiny island.

With love,

Angie

PS: We did come across Dale again before we left; the island is only 8 kilometres long and quite narrow - we even had a beer with him. Turns out the owner of the Airbnb lives in Java and hates the hospitality sector. He is thinking of closing the place down and turning it into a surf school. When I asked Dale if he knew anything about surfing, he smiled broadly and said,

"I do know quite a bit about surfing"

to: family and friends

from: Joyful Traveller

subject: Nusa Lembongan, Malaysia. Staying on a rather nice building site

Having escaped the previous Airbnb death-trap, the only place to stay nearby looked perfect on the website but there was a slight snag, it wasn't quite built yet and would not be open for a while. The lovely owner took pity on us. We could rent one of the (almost) finished cottages on the building site. We became friendly with the vast array of workmen who would make a path through to the beach for us each morning. Smiling and gesturing to the beach, happy to see us each day.

Yesterday, the owner, an amiable and sociable man, came knocking on our door. He is a local chap who has plunged his entire savings, and much of his extended family's money too, into this small complex. He is determined to make a success of it and reflecting on his quiet and kindly manner, he deserves to be.

An important festival was taking place on the beach,

"I strongly suggest for you and your husband to attend, Madam, but first we have to give you suitable attire".

We met him at the reception desk surrounded by his staff and an assortment of workmen. We were ceremoniously draped in sarongs with much enthusiastic nodding. There were looks of approval as an exquisite flower, that exactly matched the startling yellow of my outfit, was gently placed behind my ear.

By the time we arrived the beach looked as though the sun had landed and was relaxing on the shore. A mass of warm, sunshine yellow clothed people tightly packed together were waiting and talking and all so beautiful. Everyone seemed to shine, dressed in their finest clothes and huge welcoming smiles. We found a rock to perch on and in the warm glow I felt so fortunate to be in this mystical place.

Several chickens were standing by unconcerned by the events taking place, pecking at the sand. Priests arrived in their magnificent robes, flowers were strewn along the shore and then thrown out to sea. Many blessings were given. There was an air of solemnity mixed with a feeling of deep joy and gratitude. This was a local festival expressing thankfulness, and blessings were bestowed on everyone there.

I kept an eye on the chickens knowing what was to come. When it did, it was rapid and clean. The beheaded chickens lay there, offerings to the Gods and food for several families.

The importance of community, the importance of family, the importance of feeling truly grateful invaded the whole beautiful beach. They had come together to thank their Gods, to acknowledge what they had, to be blessed. Pretty magical.

With love,

Angie

to:	family and friends
from:	Joyful Traveller
subject:	Goa, India. 2018 - A bamboo hut on a beach

Hello Everyone,

Here we are in Goa, beautiful laid-back Goa - sometimes referred to as The Pearl of the Orient. From what I can make out there are two very different Goas. The North, hot spot tourist destination for those who want to party all night long and bake on the beach all day.

Then the South, filled with hippies, yoga practising, alternative spiritual beings and, if I'm honest, a bit pretentious at times.

We are in the South.

Goa is very different from much of India and it's all down to the brutal and highly ambitious Vasco de Gama who arrived on these shores in 1497. It then became a Portuguese colony for over 450 years. The Portuguese influence is everywhere: in its food, culture, religion, language and architecture.

The Portuguese brought Catholicism. Startlingly brilliant white churches stand alongside lavishly decorated Hindu temples with the occasional mosque making an appearance.

Vegetation is everywhere and appears to grow by inches overnight. Huge strangling creepers trail around anything they can get a foothold on. Coconut trees display their wares and are relieved of their burdens by lithe men who, light as a feather, shimmy up the trunks with ferocious looking machetes. Their bodies gleam in the sunshine; years of scrambling up tall palms have perfected their muscles. They are like living dynamos with the agility of monkeys. I watch them and, with my neurotic mind, wonder how many of them have fallen, maybe to their death. Then, I wonder if they were to fall would they fall on top of me? So I move smartly out of the way, surveying them from a distance.

Beauty is everywhere. The highly coloured painted houses reminiscent of Portuguese village dwellings, sit tumbling down. This is a harsh environment and paint is needed every year, but paint is expensive, so buildings take on the patina of water. Patterns are made each year and houses patched up and still stand. The deep red earth contrasts with the green fields. Henna tattoos, intricate, filigree creations spiral along human arms and, for some reason, make me feel happy looking at them.

The beach is a source of wonder - a vast assortment of human life. It's a joy to watch boys playing cricket. They set themselves up on a flat part of the beach, late afternoon. It is a serious affair mixed with pleasure and enjoyment.

Hippies, artists, free thinkers and soul searchers find their way to the South after the acid and MDMA from the North have taken their toll. Recovering wild folk who wouldn't even let a humble aspirin defile their now so pure bodies, disciples to yoga and alternative medicines. As serious yoga devotees, they practice every day, early morning. Getting into unreasonable looking poses at times with that look on their faces,

"Watch me, I am so very fit and supple, and you are not". I am being a bit mean, but some of them do have that air of superiority. I wish just once they might trip up on their multicoloured scarves.

Yoga is a serious affair here. Dozens of classes take place taught by enlightened, fervent teachers. It becomes difficult not to get caught up with the idea that something could, and often does, change a person's life. I go regularly. My stiff limbs seem more pliable and my posture maybe a little less stooped, but I am pretty hopeless alongside all the taut-limbed, honed-to-perfection bodies which stretch alongside me.

The ubiquitous pashmina is a sought-after item and can often be found nestling in amongst vegetables or canned foods and constipation tablets. All who sell them put up large notices proclaiming, 'Real pashminas'. A 'real' pashmina is a highly expensive piece of clothing made from the belly of a Mongolian goat. Amongst the hundreds of pashminas for sale in the beachfront shops of Goa I doubt if there is a 'real' pashmina among them.

Cheesecloth garments are still for sale. They hang from make-shift awnings, adding to the 60s mellow, laid back vibe. Men with shoulder length hair encased around head bands are a nod to the Flower Power time.

Sandalwood mixed with spices, cow dung and highly perfumed flowers compete for your olfactory senses. It is heady and powerful, creating a heavy and dreamy mood. For a moment I can be one of those laid-back old hippies dismissing any worries or problems - just for a moment.

A few yards away, the jungle encroaches on the beach and with it those naughty monkeys. Ever vigilant and aware of countless pairs of eyes, I take a stick with me while I walk. In the mistaken belief I will be spared, I am not: they come near me baring their teeth and chattering, longing to rip my bag from my shoulder and remove my straw hat. I square up to them and stare. I get the distinct impression they don't regard me as an innocent tourist and bound back to their sentry duties on the tree branches. No easy pickings this time.

Here, there is a sense of impermanence, of nature taking back control. Many of these beach shacks, cafés and small hotels are temporary structures often made from wooden packing cases and containers which must be dismantled at the end of the summer in readiness for the monsoons. These rainstorms come every year, try their hardest to lay everything bare.

We have a hut on the beach. It is made out of palms and held up with bamboo poles. A small balcony with a couple of wonky plastic chairs surrounds the place. The roof has an assortment of wildlife living in the creepers; we hear them each night. Only yards from the waves, it is soporific and quite magical.

Most days a procession of large cows make their slow, almost hypnotic journey to this skewwhiff home of ours. The first day we wondered why a large rectangle piece of wood was left outside, perched precariously by the entrance to the little terrace. We soon found out. Nudging their noses onto our cracked windowpane early the next morning, were three huge white cows.

They still visit each day but now stand outside, they can't quite climb over the carefully positioned bit of old wood, we now know what to do with. I don't feed them, we all acknowledge each other, say Good Morning then they troop off in search of more generous tourists.

The dogs are a delight, a source of amusement and utterly endearing. Only a cold-hearted soul could not fall for their charms. They know how to pull the heart strings as they contort themselves on the beach each day. Maybe they've taken up yoga. Some lie sprawled out in Childs Pose; others look like they are deep into a meditation. They have this benign quality about them, and all seem to rub along together. Packs of them saunter beside the beach, playing in the sand, an occasional dip in the sea. Seemingly to accept what life has given them, happy with their lot.

There is no hot water. At first, I thought maybe that was the problem, I could never feel quite clean enough and my skin started to take on the look of one of the reptiles that keep us company from a vantage point on the ceiling each night. My hair looks exactly like an English haystack and my face has that weather-beaten look which so many older ex-pats seem to have. One day I suddenly realised the water was sea water. Hundreds of pounds worth of expensive face creams wasted; should have keep my money.

Kept

I asked our very genial host, Sandeep, if I could have a few coat hangers. He happily agreed with my request and came back a few days later with a chain which he dangled from a joint in the ceiling and a couple of bent, wire coat hangers to hang through the links. These were so mangled they refused to behave. Everything is now crammed into my suitcase and emerges creased beyond recognition but in the heat and humidity the creases seem to miraculously disappear. The mangled coat hangers are permanently attached to the hanging chain which we constantly keep whacking into. I often ask Sandeep if he can move it, he has yet to do that.

Sandeep and I have become buddies. He likes to chat. Every day he appears with a little gift, a mango or a few flowers or maybe a bunch of bananas. We have a delightful little ceremony where he hands over his gifts and I interrogate him. He seems happy with this arrangement and I am delighted as he's a wonderful gossip. I get to hear about his past guests and their little foibles.

He worked as a deckhand on cruise liners for half his life. When he became unwell after thirty-odd years of service, they sacked him. No pension or sick pay. Odious companies catering for a rich, spoilt public. He didn't show much anger or resentment while he told me this. He shrugged his shoulders,

"That is what life is sometimes Angeeee, what do you do?"

I meanwhile, was jumping up and down, feeling hateful and furious on his behalf.

"Angeeeee" (my name was becoming longer the more he tried to console me), "I have my family, I have my house and I live here". He said this as he gazed out towards the azure sea, the golden sands and the gently lapping waves.

He's got a point.

Sandeep is not too keen on the Russians. I am hoping it is because of a language barrier and a different way of speaking, but I'm not sure. It's stupid and ignorant to generalise but some of them do have an unfortunate way about them. The other day I was wandering around the local market when a lady approached me, offering flowers for sale. I smiled and politely declined shaking my head. She was surprised, stood back and said, "You no Russian lady, good" and promptly placed a bright orange flower behind my ear.

In the next hut to us lives a large Russian lady. She appears each year from the cold of Moscow bossing Sandeep around demanding various appliances, none of which he supplies. She materialises in the Spring and departs in late Autumn. I've tried in vain to engage her in conversation but she's not too interested. Each day a gaggle of elderly Russian ladies gather outside her hut. They talk, they shout, they knit, they eat. Vast amounts of food are laid out on rickety tables which groan and threaten to collapse. Huge plates of meat, mountains of potatoes, and not a green bean in sight. The food starts disappearing on the dot of 1pm and not a scrap is left in the empty dishes. Bosoms the size of small mountains jiggle up and down encased in vast swimsuits and arms like hams gesture in the air.

These ladies are similar to the Babushkas I met years ago. When I had Moscow stopovers during the 'Cold War', the crew stayed in hotels resembling prison blocks. Huge affairs, every room identical, resembling poor youth hostels. Each floor had a keeper-of-the-keys. A monstruous lady, whose face had forgotten how to smile. With a mixture of disdain and outright belligerence she would hand over a room key, a toilet roll, a thin, rough towel and a small bar of soap. We nicknamed them the "Dragon Ladies".

Sandeep is bemused as he can't quite make us out, we are not his usual guests,

"Nice hotels along the beach, they have cold and hot running of water".

I reassure him of how happy we are here and besides, I say, "We wouldn't get to have our little get togethers if we were in a fancy hotel, would we Sandeep?"

He's not convinced but leaves happy, maybe he's deciding what nice little treat he can bring for us tomorrow.

I'm off now; found a dear little yoga class with a smiling and serene Frenchman. He gently teases my stiff limbs into place. His accent is hypnotic and last week I managed to fall asleep while we were supposed to be meditating. I think I might have been snoring on the mat, I hope not. I know he will still smile that beatific smile when I try and glide in today and I'll pretend I'm super fit, super agile and super together and, of course, pigs might fly......

With love,

Angie

to: family and friends

from: Joyful Traveller

subject: Goa, India - An encounter with a certain doctor

Dear Ones,

I had an encounter with an Ayurvedic doctor. It came at exactly the right time, as though someone up there had engineered this meeting.

I had been advised to seek out this man. A friendly face in a yoga class began chatting as we moved our contorted bodies off the mats. I grimaced a little then dismissed my ailment as 'a bit of arthritis', that seems to cover nicely any problems one encounters as aging kicks in. She reassured me this didn't need to be so and promptly gave me the name of a doctor who lived up a dirt track, in the jungle part of the island.

I made up my mind I had to visit him but didn't want to navigate the path on my own, so I persuaded my long-suffering Scotsman to accompany me. We trekked through the undergrowth; seemed like hours, mindful of snakes and aware of bands of monkeys monopolising the trees. They stared down with bad-tempered faces, undecided whether they wanted a confrontation.

Eventually, we came across a building deep in the jungle. An elegant, soft, stone house glimmered in the dappled light. Navigating the steep stairs down to the entrance, we were met by a tinkling fountain in a pretty courtyard. Pots of overflowing flowers and secret places where teak chairs with silk cushions nestled. Peace and quiet and contentment pervaded this place. We sat happily in the dappled shade and waited.

The appointment was made just for me. Kenneth was adamant he didn't want a consultation when I suggested it. Then, this vison appeared: a yogi, strong, powerful and in complete command. I found this definition of a yogi,

'To be a yogi means to live without the coffins that other people build around them'.

He seemed rooted in the earth but with a part of him which was somewhere else. Years of demanding yoga practice had honed his body to a perfect state. He demanded attention just by simply standing in the space around him. The air seemed stilled, another source at work here. He drifted past me and stood in front of Kenneth who made no sign of uneasiness. The yogi-doctor wafted his hand and Kenneth followed.

An hour later Kenneth emerged looking pleased and tranquil.

Then it was my turn and I found myself sitting in front of a huge teak table with the doctor sat opposite. In Ayurvedic medicine the doctor first has to determine what your Dosha is. There are three types of Dosha: Kapha, Vata and Pitta representing, Earth, Wind, and Fire.

Kapha is of the earth, and this is Kenneth's Dosha. Grounded, dependable, calm and peace loving (the complete opposite to me).

Ayurvedic medicine is over 3,000 years old, one of the most ancient of medicines. It turned out that this doctor had trained for seven years and had worked extensively in Europe.

My Dosha was Pitta; no question, of course, fire. He gave me some recommendations about eating, exercising and calcium intake but then he said,

"What is your profession, Angela?"

I puffed up my chest and perhaps looked rather pleased with myself,

"Oh, I've just trained as a counsellor".

He looked long and hard at me, the sort of look that infiltrates your soul and I started to get hot and uncomfortable. I did a bit of squirming around in the chair that started creaking - reflecting my discomfiture. I'm not quite sure how long he observed me for, it seemed like an eternity.

He then swiftly shut the notebook he had been writing in,

"Give it up, it is no good for you. It will not make you happy, damaging to your well-being, stop now".

He stood up and continued talking as he made his way to the door,

"You are not suited to it, never would be, far too emotional" (read neurotic, highly strung, tending towards unbalanced behaviour - that's not what he said but that's how I was interpreting his remarks).

"You are of The Fire variety, this work will do nothing but burn you out".

I sat there not wanting to get up and follow him out, feeling an enormous amount of animosity towards him. Kenneth said I emerged with a face like thunder. I could hardly bring myself to look at him as we said goodbye. I wanted to ask more but somehow, he had said it all.

He bowed, we bowed, he murmured 'Namaste' and then,

"Angela, go to the beach now, walk on your own, be at peace, seek the truth".

I did that. I walked along the beach and as I walked, I realised he was utterly and completely right. All the dear, damaged souls I had seen, I wanted to fix. I wanted to patch them up and find a way to repair them. A wise therapist does not do that. I remembered years ago I had attended a group interview to be a Samaritan. I was turned down. Highly indignant, I called them. How could they turn me down with all my experience, maybe they had mixed me up with someone else? I was that confident about my skills. No, there was no mix up. I learnt that I could never allow a suicide victim to throw themselves off a bridge. I'd be there hanging on to their ankles trying to persuade them otherwise, trying to fix them, when maybe that would be the last thing they would want.

Namaste.

With love,

Angie

The journey started as we left our hut on the beach in Goa. By the time the taxi eventually appeared - forty-five minutes late - we were not exactly that relaxed.

"Terrible hold up there was", said the driver who had come from the next village where there were only a handful of tuk-tuks and a few motorbikes on the road at any one time. He stood by the side of his beaten-up contraption. Possibly a white coloured vehicle in a previous life; now it was covered in layers of dust and various cow pats.

"Madam, I will get you to the airport in jolly right time". And with that, we were hurled into the streets.

For the entire journey he wouldn't let a millimetre come between him and any unfortunate car in front of him, braking frantically and one hand permanently pressed on the horn. At times, waving to the driver in front, he took both hands off the steering wheel.

I clutched a sick bag frantically screaming at Kenneth to tell this lunatic driver to slow down. Kenneth, who likes to take everything in his stride, was definitely looking queasy. As he lent forwards, I noticed his shirt was covered in sweat. The seats were made of squelchy plastic, the temperature over a hundred degrees.

Goa airport that day was reminiscent of being in a really bad dream. Hordes of people all milling round walking frenetically, all very busy, all very loud, and hundreds of men in army-type uniforms trying to look important and authoritarian. They took so long looking at the passport and then looking at the ticket then back to the passenger. Their eyes going backwards and forwards in a continual dance. As a result, it was not uncommon for travellers to miss their flights.

How some of Air India's planes ever leave the ground, with passengers I have no idea. We stood in the standby queue surrounded by dozens and dozens of harassed looking passengers: no one seemed to know what was happening. The check-in lady hiding behind her desk seemed to be in the same category as the security staff. She either kept a blank expression on her face or she would shout at some unfortunate soul trying to check-in.

A kind looking man was standing in the throng. I felt he had the look of someone who might know how the system worked; this incomprehensible standby system.

I was right; he was a loading officer for Air India based in Mumbai and loved to fly with British Airways. He made it his mission to get us on the flight. He found out after lots of wringing of hands and stern language that, indeed, there were no seats on this flight to Mumbai, but another flight had been delayed and it looked more hopeful. We got on.

We're now at Mumbai airport.

We collected our bags, always a huge relief to see those bags coming down the conveyor belt. Standby bags are shoved on at the last moment and notorious for not being seen again for a long time, if ever. Now, all we had to do was to negotiate the security staff so we could get into the departure lounge for our flight to London.

We didn't have the required stamp; he wouldn't let us in. We tried in vain to explain the check-in staff won't give us a stamp as we have standby tickets, we have to go directly to the gate. He continued to stare at us refusing to listen, obsessing about a stamp which we cannot get as standby passengers. We again showed him our standby tickets and our passports. He stared through us. I knew we had to get through. I knew we could be here in this airport until we grew very old. I knew something drastic had to be done.

There was now a huge crowd of disgruntled passengers behind us, things were turning nasty. Kenneth and I looked at each other and decided to go for it. As he stood there shaking his head from side to side and repeatedly saying, "Madam, stand aside", I told him with a voice reminiscent of a bossy headmistress, "We are going to the departure lounge and that's that".

We barged past him. We knew he had a gun and we raced for the lifts not daring to look back, our hearts thumping and our faces red and dripping with panicked sweat. In the departure lounge we became conscious of every security chap lurking around thinking that any minute now someone is going to grab us - but they didn't. After all that, we had to wait for another four hours until we were called to the standby queue.

We get Club seats, we are so happy. We nonchalantly walk to the gate and go through a short queue at security as we are Club passengers, the exclusive ones who have reclining beds and yummy food to eat and gin and tonics and champagne and posh eye shades secreted in goody bags. Nine and a half wonderful hours of luxury. We will arrive in London as fresh as a daisy ready for the next leg of our trip.

There's an old expression, one that Kenneth repeats every single time we travel on standby,

"The wheels aren't up yet" no, but I'm confidently clutching my precious Club seat Boarding Pass and I'm in the exclusive boarding line. I get to the desk.

"No, you have to wait, Madam, go now back to your seat we haven't called your seat number yet", and the check-in chap dismissed me with an imperious wave of his hand.

Me smiling, "Yes you have, look it's 5b"

He took my Boarding Pass and fed the number into his computer and with an irritated edge to his voice said,

"Madam, your seat has been changed, you now have the jump seat".

Those chilling words - words no staff traveller ever wants to hear, 'jump seat'.

Including a delay of an hour and a half on the ground, I sat for over ten hours as a toilet monitor. A 'jump seat', I might have mentioned before, is a fold-down, postage-stamp-size seat used by the crew during take-off and landing. My 'jump seat' was at the back of the aircraft next to the back door and adjacent to the toilets. A certain percentage of passengers have never left India and, very often, this is their first flight.

The loo doors can be really confusing. Some doors fold inwards when you push them and others open outwards. I couldn't just sit there and watch these travellers struggle, so I would stretch forward in my 'jump seat' and push or pull the toilet door. Several times I got a tip, maybe some passengers thought, how wonderful it was to have toilet attendants on BA flights.

We landed, having had no sleep for days, but I had met some lovely passengers. Some had even offered me their seat for a few hours. That was probably when I started looking slightly green around the gills and my mouth had turned a purple colour with the cold. The unkind air-conditioning gathers around that tiny little crew seat and refuses to budge.

Home safe and sound now.

With love,

Angie

Hello Everyone,

Here we are in Mount Forest, Southern Ontario.

I met Liz at our local Further Education College after I had been asked to leave my school; a dull, pretentious, all-girls private school. She also had to leave her equally dull, all-girls private school. Her parents had run out of money, no more left for extortionate school fees. I suppose it was inevitable that we would find each other. Our aim was to meet as many boys as possible, to drink as much cheap cider as we could throw down our throats and to start to live. For three years I took and re-took exams while Lizzy went off to train as a nurse. Then, she met Simon and deserted me. I was her only bridesmaid. She shot off with her Welsh doctor husband to the wilds of Canada and this is where we are now, looking after Winston, their endearing, loveable Retriever.

Wheat, corn and soya crops stretch as far as the eye can see - spread out over thousands of acres, huge skies and flat lands and Mennonites. I've been here before but only for a fleeting visit. This time we are here for a month and I decided I had to try and go to a Mennonite Meeting. I was so determined and even when Lizzy's daughter said it wouldn't happen, I refused to listen. Meetings were for Mennonites.

Lizzy and Simon left for England and I smartly nipped round to their neighbour, Miriam. Miriam is a local Mennonite schoolteacher. She is kind and gracious and if she felt uncomfortable with this stranger knocking on her door, she never let on.

We stood on the porch talking. It was really me doing all the talking and Miriam smiling her delightful, kind, benevolent smile - a smile I would love to have. I'm now trying to cultivate one; it doesn't come easy. It's that grace and kindly nature that shines through. But, by the time I left, I had secured an invitation to next Sunday's Meeting.

It's a fascinating community. There's lots wrong with it, of course there is, but there's also countless things right with it. A fast-growing community, exceptional in this day and age, with few who want to leave.

Mennonites, similar to Quakers, loathed the idolatry of the Catholic church. They are part of the Anabaptist movement of the 16th Century Reformation. They wanted a simpler, gentler way of worship. They also rejected the baptism of babies and the practise of "Indulgences". Babies don't have a choice but adults do. Only adults are baptised. "Indulgences" started in ancient times but gained momentum when Pope Leo the 10th decided he wanted to rebuild St Peter's Basilica. Unfortunately for him, he didn't have the dosh so he pushed these "Indulgences" meaning that if you paid the church a nice big healthy sum of money, you'd spend less time in purgatory.

There are deeply conservative Mennonites and also progressive ones.

The Mennonites here are of a Conservative Order and I am completely fascinated by them. They have no cars, televisions, or computers and in many cases, no electricity. They are now allowed to own tractors (they're mainly farmers) and, quite recently, a telephone. Leave school at fourteen and work the land. Have loads of children and bake delicious cakes. Women wear long dresses covered from their throats to their ankles with material very similar to old Laura Ashly prints. A bonnet covers their uncut hair. Their black, horse-drawn buggies resemble Victorian carriages; black horses fly through the air. So strange to see cars and trucks parked alongside horses and buggies which are tethered to iron railings in supermarket car parks. *Ashley*

What on earth could I wear on Sunday? Rummaged through Liz's wardrobe, found a roomy navy shift dress, black tights, flat shoes and a headscarf. Looked nothing like a Mennonite but felt

I wouldn't cause offence and, duly, set off with Miriam in the rain.

On the way she explained it would be a two-hour service in Pennsylvanian German. The Mennonites originated from Northern Europe and have managed to keep their unique language. Dear Miriam, in her hand was a little bible alongside a hymn book written in English. She was hoping I could follow parts of the service but, as it turned out, I wouldn't need either.

Females congregated and entered on one side of the building, males on the other. Lots of laughing and chatting, everyone trying their best not to stare at me as we waited in the women's section of the Meeting House. We filed into a plain, large, warm wood room, no electricity. A deep sense of peace was palpable, almost mesmeric. Babies and children sat in silence, in silence! Over two hundred Mennonites were quietly seated. I became deeply aware of what a privilege it was for me to be sitting there. The singing started, unaccompanied. It was like an unpleasant dirge but as it continued I got accustomed to it and found it lulled me into a quiet, contented state. I could even hum along a little while reading the English translation.

Four ministers, dressed in sombre black suits, sat in front of us on a high wooden plinth, each taking turns to speak. The first sermon began. I became captivated; being of service, helping others, a life of simplicity and great thanks. It was beautiful, as was the rest of the ministry. Halfway through it suddenly dawned on me. I'd been so caught up with the experience of being there, it sounds ridiculous, but I now realised the service was all in English.

It all came to an end and before we filed out, I turned to Miriam,

"Miriam, the service was in English, not in your Pennsylvanian German language"

"Yes" she says and then shyly adds, "They knew you were coming".

Over two hundred folk had to sit through a two-hour service not in their own language, all because I was there.

I've told Kenneth that if he starts acting like an old fart, I'm off - with a headscarf and a bible tucked under my arm.

With love,

Angie x

Miriam, in the softest of voices said,

"Would you care to teach a lesson one day, Angie?".

Without batting an eyelid, I said I would love to. Then it dawned on me how different and how careful I would have to be not to cause offence.

"What sort of things would the children be interested in Miriam?

"We like to learn about flowers, Angie, and trees and wildlife; what crops are grown in your country and maybe what popular dishes you have".

There was no such thing as a projector and, of course, no computers.

I set about hunting for images of home on the Internet and found some lovely stuff:

Bright yellow daffodils, purple and pink tulips; photographs of English roses, dog wood roses, climbing roses, big flouncy ones, tiny miniature ones; grey squirrels cavorting among trees; deer in woodland and foxes attacking rubbish bins in the city; old oak trees, graceful silver birches and weeping willows by running streams; combine harvesters in wheat fields, startling yellow rapeseed growing under an early summer sun, fields of cabbages and corn; robins in snow covered fields, thrushes and magpies feeding at bird tables and snowy owls perched on telegraph wires; fish and chips with mushy peas and Sarson's vinegar; a china teapot, teacup and saucer and a milk jug alongside a plate of digestive biscuits.

A particularly accommodating chap in the local print shop helped me turn all these colourful images into large, heavy-duty cards.

He was intrigued, he hadn't known of any stranger going into a Mennonite school to give a lesson before.

Armed with my photo cards, hoping they would interest the children, I arrived at the school. I also had good old English tea (we always travel with a box of English Breakfast teabags) and I'd managed to track down some Paterson's Real Scottish Shortbread Fingers which would accompany a photo of The Scotsman in his kilt.

The school is made from warm wood, inviting, cosy and simple. Ageless desks with fold down lids and little ink wells and wooden chairs with slatted backs. A heavy pine desk sits at the front of the room with a blackboard that covers the wall behind. On the board had been pinned a map of the world with a sticker showing Great Britain, it looked so small and insignificant, this tiny island land.

All I was conscious of when I walked into the room was the goodwill emanating from Miriam and the children. It was a sea of smiling, eager faces. They stood up quickly followed by a welcoming hymn, sung in their language.

As they sat down all eyes were on me, waiting expectantly. The girls were sat in neat rows on one side of the room. With their white prayer bonnets set on the back of their heads, flowery dresses under dark coloured pinafores. Gleaming hair tied back in pigtails or neat plaits and wide-open faces.

The boys in short trousers and braces, hair looking like someone had plonked a pudding basin on top of their head and cut around it, scrubbed hands and fresh complexions.

There was lots of interest in every picture I showed them. They couldn't believe our miserable amount of snowfall. They regularly have four months when everything is blanketed under heavy snow drifts.

I was a bit pathetic when they started to ask me about various farming methods. The boys leave school at fourteen and usually work the land on the family farm, fulltime. Girls mostly work in the home, cooking, sewing, tending vegetable gardens and then often marrying and producing large families. Community is one of the most important aspect of their lives. It keeps them together, nurtures them, protects them. There was a sense of light-hearted fun.

Around the room were pictures of the natural world, beautiful photos of animals, mountains, trees and flowers.

Everything was mightily old-fashioned, transporting me back to my time as a schoolgirl in an antiquated Victorian building. Neat rows of desks, a blackboard with real chalk, a milk monitor and a list of jobs each pupil was allocated to do. Once, I remember being allowed to clean the blackboard and can still feel that sense of importance which swept over me as I cleaned away. It seemed an easier time then. I'm being fanciful now but there was something hugely refreshing about these children. No secret mobile phones hidden under the desk. No social media and body shaming. Looking around, I couldn't imagine any of them having eating issues or an obsession about what they looked like.

There are bound to be things wrong with this community, of course, but that morning I could appreciate what family, community, a common faith and love, appreciation and understanding of the natural world, what gifts those truly are.

Towards the end of the lesson, we all had a cup of English Breakfast tea and a shortbread biscuit as I explained to them about the Scotsman's traditional national dress.

As I left, the children were in the playground. The girls had changed out of their white bonnets into heavier outdoor ones and were sitting on the steps eating their packed lunches laughing and chatting with the boys who were trying to push each other off the steps.

They all got up and waved like mad as I left in the enormous four-by-four with built-in phone, navigation system, radio, heated seats and my mobile phone which was nagging me with missed calls.

I think we could have much to learn from the Mennonite community. I know I feel enriched by having been one tiny part of it, even for just one morning.

With love,

Angie

PS: I just remembered; I must tell you about my buggy ride. A lovely Mennonite fellow with a splendid horse and buggy offered to take Kenneth and I for a ride.

We flew through the air on a beautiful sunny day. It was magical, exhilarating, dashing past wide-open fields, able to see everything nature had to offer. Sitting in an open buggy with the wind whipping my headscarf and Kenneth hanging onto his Panama hat. A jet-black horse that didn't need to be given any directions. The rider and horse appeared, at times, to be as one. No evil emissions, no pollution and the horse poo would be used to cultivate the vegetable gardens. It was all quite joyous.

to: family and friends

from: Joyful Traveller

subject: New Orleans, Louisiana 2019 - The Big Easy

Hello all you Lovelies,

We are now in the Deep South, in New Orleans. It's a wild, exciting, crazy place, unlike anywhere else in America. Perched on the banks of the Mississippi and Lake Pontchartrain, it was a prize possession for invaders. The French founded it in 1718. The Spanish then grabbed it from the French and the French wrestled it back again. After all that it became part of The United States of America.

Referred to as The Big Easy and, yes, locals often say "now y'all take it easy". A way of saying have a good time wrapped around a warning. It's a laid back, informal city but it can be a violent one. The disparity between those who have and those who have not is vast.

Life seems to be bigger here, more colourful, more vibrant. Music shapes this city's uniqueness. Walking around the old French Quarter, sounds spill out onto the pavements. They mix with the smells of "beignets" (sweet pastries) and creole cooking. This is a city that welcomes with arms wide open aspiring musicians and struggling jazz and blues performers. A trail of bars offers awe inspiring music. You can hop from one to another and never be disappointed. It's immediate, it engulfs you, your feet start to tap and your spirits rise and here you feel alive.

The architecture in the famous French Quarter is lovely to look at. Intricately woven wrought iron balconies vie with dangling hanging baskets whose contents spill out, cascading down almost to the road. Stuffed with ferns whose fronds are burnished by the sun leaving them looking like fragile works of art. The Spanish left their mark here. Beautiful colonial houses, tall, upright, romantic architecture at its finest.

Guy arrived for a few days and it's been the greatest joy to be here with him. Not his first visit, he had meticulously researched everything about this fabulous city a few years before. He has this tremendous energy which surrounds him, and a desire to experience as much as he can. His love of this city and the people here, is infectious and ignites our imagination, and we learn much.

Tennessee Williams called New Orleans his spiritual home. It was here he wrote 'A Streetcar Named Desire'.

The streetcars here inspire devotion, adored by locals and tourists alike. They trundle along weaving their way quite magically through the city streets. They are part of the very fabric of this city. As you sit on the heavy, worn, rich mahogany seats, with their shining brass fittings, you could be in a film; one with lots of romance. It's a bit like when you wear vintage clothes, there's a tangible link to the past.

The other day while riding a streetcar a fellow passenger started chatting. He was a teacher on his way home. I mentioned how friendly everyone had been and asked him why that could be.

"Well, Ma'am it's almost rude not to talk to your fellow passenger on a streetcar".

It's a cheerful mixture of old-fashioned manners and a desire to find out more about people. Happily for me, it was a longish journey and he seemed to want to keep chatting. Eventually my tram stop came into sight,

"Well little lady, I could listen to that voice of yours all day long, it's like a soft melody".

He was so kind and as we journeyed, he had insisted on writing down a list of the best music bars along with mouth-watering descriptions of delicious food and secret eating places that only locals would know. A few days later, that Southern kindness surfaced again.

We were lost, wandering around the backstreets. The Scotsman refused to ask for directions, clinging to his map and informing me he knew exactly where we were heading, but I knew he didn't. So, we trudged on and on with me getting hotter and more bothered. I then threw a bit of a wobbly right there on the pavement. With that, my guardian angel appeared. She was sat in her car laughing her head off and as she did huge gold earrings bobbed uncontrollably up and down. She was wearing the most stunning multicoloured kaftan, topped off with a complicated turban. Her deep southern voice carried across the street.

"What you gettin' so riddled up about Misses? Where you going? Hop in, I'll give you folks a ride".

And so we did. She was generous and kind and the most wonderful company.

"Where y'all from? I watch that Downtown Abbey; you sounds a bit like one of those folks".

Downton Abbey, the BBC television series, is huge in The States, everyone seems to watch it. It was the second top-rated show after the Super Bowl.

"I hope the folks here have been looking after you?" She was a black woman, a New Orleanian, and she was very keen to know what we thought of her city, especially the people we had met.

"We love it", we said in unison.

Food then became the main topic of our conversation. It was her passion and she wanted to find out what dishes we had eaten. Food is what binds people together here. They talk about it, they argue about it, they dream about it. I described the dishes we had already eaten: gumbo, crawfish étouffée, jambalaya, mouth-wateringly delectable rice dishes - all prepared with secret ingredients known only to the chef. I went on to tell her about the fried chicken which was so good I was too impatient to use a knife and fork and just stuffed it into my mouth, letting butter drip down onto my clothes. Then, of course, there's crawfish, which drove us mad trying to unlock the insides. Only a Louisianan can master this art I was told. By the end of the journey we had exchanged recipes and our thoughts about God and life.

I emerged from the car a little sad, I wanted to stay all day with her. Her love of life and food, her faith and this city was infectious. I wanted a bit of it to rub off onto me.

It turned out she was a taxi driver. When we went to pay for our ride, she point-blank refused to accept a penny,

"Hey honey, if I ever get to go to your country, be sure there will be someone there that will do a little kindness for me, that's how it works. God bless you and take it easy now".

I said a little prayer as we left her, hoping that if she ever did get to Britain her kindness would indeed be repaid.

With love,

Angie

Hello Lovelies,

Farm-sitting now, and I'm not that far away from home. It's only West Wales but feels like another country, and of course it is.

Remember the TV programme, The Good Life? Was always under the illusion that I could be another Felicity Kendal. I bought the designer wellies and a rather nifty pair of dungarees, that's where it ends.

You go through a dear little Welsh town where everyone seems to speak to everyone else. Herds of tractors race along the High Street carrying smiling farmers with red cheeks, and a latent desire to be racing-car drivers. There are quaint dress shops selling flowery frocks and elasticated, waisted trousers behind ancient nicotine-coloured plastic, which veils the shop window contents from the sun. This casts a strange yellow hue over all the merchandise.

Everyone seems to know Nessie, "Ohhhh, a gorgeous girl" and Robbie, "Oh yes, oh yes the cheese maker, and a fine one at that".

A few miles away and you navigate yourself down a tiny winding dirt track. Two miles of rutted, potholed, mayhem to the farm.

I often seem to arrive when cows are passing through, ambling from one field to another. They have a right-of-way over the track that goes down to the farm.

Dafydd appears on his ancient quad bike: a bike held together by bits of frayed rope and duct tape. He cajoles his herd of black and white milkers into the field. Cows are curious animals; this lot is no exception. They pass by with a nonchalant air, trying to convey the impression they aren't interested in you. Then, you see them having a sneaky look, they just can't help themselves. Some of the braver ones come to a standstill right in front of me. They scrutinise me with a mixture of suspicion and intrigue.

The farmer, Dafydd, has that ruddy complexion, years spent in the outdoors battling many cold and dismal winters. He has the kindest cornflower-blue eyes and seems to take great delight when we pass the time of day with each other. Standing in the lane, we chat like old friends.

We've covered most areas of life, including holidays and Brexit (about which he's terribly concerned).

"Do you get to go away much, Dafydd, with all your farming commitments?"

"Oh yes, we had a day out at the Royal Welsh Show a few weeks back". Another world.

One of our talks led to my Welsh heritage,

"I'm a quarter Welsh, Dafydd".

"Well, you're almost one of us then, aren't you?"

He wanted to know more. When I told him the story of my great grandfather, he became even more captivated and tells me he is going to, "ask around, someone will know something, be sure of that".

My Great Grandfather, a miner from Aberaeron, up the road from here, made a huge fortune in bird-poo. Shipped it from some distant land, sold it to farmers as a fertilizer. Unfortunately, my wonderful but wayward grandparents blew the lot. The trusted Nanny Blackstone managed to salvage all my Grandmother's designer dresses and shoved them under the mattress before the bailiffs arrived. My glorious Nana without a penny to her name continued to dress in Dior and Givenchy.

Back to the farm. After this somewhat challenging journey you arrive at the house. It looks like one of those cottages that adorn old biscuit tins. Three-foot thick walls, stone floors, wooden beams and tiny windows that let in little slivers of light. Records date back to 1602 when it was reported to be a Drovers resting place. It's dark and dismal and I'm a bit scared there, but it also has a mysterious charm.

Four lovely entertaining dogs who we have become very fond of: two overweight smelly Labradors, an ankle-biter and a whippet-cross called Basil. Basil is the 'ratter'. Official duties are sniffing out and grabbing rats by the neck. He's kept very busy. Unfortunately, their baskets live in the kitchen, three under the huge table and one next to the Aga. I've now taken to wearing a scarf tied around my neck with organic tea tree oil generously sprinkled onto it. The smell of farm dogs is somewhat unappetizing. When I take them up to the top field every day for a little wander and to count the sheep, they have a glorious time rolling in the sheep poo.

One of the cats is a Maine Coon. These cats have beautiful long coats that need to be brushed religiously every day. This one looks as though it has never even seen a brush. She's taken on the appearance of an old mop, the type made out of rope, and wanders around the place, even scaring the dogs. I long to groom her but just can't bring myself to do it. Festus, the dark and brooding tabby, usually brings home a selection of small furry rodents every night with entrails smeared across the shower room floor as presents for Kenneth in the morning.

Walter, the magnificent cockerel starts his day, and ours, at 4.30 each morning. He makes the most extraordinary racket as he marshals his lady friends into the bushes just under our window.

There are two sets of pigs, quarter ton Hungarian boars the old girls in the nearest field get fed first, then the chickens - dozens of them dotted all over the place, then it's the turn of the goats.

Napoleon, the horned Billy goat, looks ferocious but he's frightened of his own shadow. With his curly horns and long beard he's a real softie. Cedric is our favourite. Kenneth is still fond of him even though on the second day he jumped up and knocked his tooth out. Kenneth now looks like a demented farmer. He dare not go to the barbers, there's some very suspect haircuts here so his hair skims his shoulders, his beard is grey and grizzly and he's missing a front tooth.

Once the goats have eaten, the fun begins. I have to stand with a broom and Kenneth opens the gate to the field. There's a sort of game that gets played every day. The goats try to escape and eat the rose bushes and we try and manoeuvre them into the field where they should be going. We eventually win, then it's repeated all over again at the end of the day.

Atchoo and Hapu, the other two Hungarian boars, are the last to be fed. Hapu turns out to be a bit of a Houdini character. The first time he escaped, Kenneth was on his own tending to the garden. He could feel something nuzzling his legs. Thinking it was one of the Labradors he didn't take much notice until he started to smell something even more unpleasant. He glanced down and there was Hapu, the Hungarian boar, snuggling up to him.

In the Scotsman's calm and ever composed manner, he managed to lure him back into his compound with tasty little treats, and then summoned Nessie who smartly whipped round to help seal up the hole. They didn't do a particularly good job as a week later Hapu appeared by my side, grinning, teeth the size of tombstones dancing up and down, a snout that could smell the sheep food I was dishing out. I laid a trail which he happily followed back to his home and then I stood screaming for

Kenneth to help fix the hole before he could make another bolt for freedom.

He still looks at me and as he does I know what he's thinking,

"Just you watch out, I'm planning my next escape". I'm feeding him lots of juicy leftovers just in case he does, so he might feel kindly disposed towards me. That fence still looks very dubious.

This is quite a crazy housesitting experience but Guy summed it up a few days ago,

"You love the drama Ma" - and he's probably right.

With love,

Angie

Finally......

The beloved Scotsman has recently found out he has a rather nasty form of Parkinson's.

This means our life will change. No more sleeping in dodgy bamboo huts, walking up steep hillsides, or running for stand-by seats.

I know it's a cliché but what I've learnt from putting these emails together is that we have to grab every opportunity that comes our way.

I'm so grateful that we were able to do all that rather chaotic, unorganised, exciting travelling when we could. That old saying 'You never know what's around the corner', proves to be true.

That's not to say it's going to stop us, it will just be a gentler, easier way of travelling.

Actually, I've got my next book on the horizon; thinking of calling it, 'Travels Around a Trusty Walking Stick'.

Until then,

With love,

Angie

Thank you......

I have too many members of my family and enthusiastic friends to mention here; those of you who have encouraged me to publish this book, I hope you know who you are.

Alison Powell at Write Club who tried to turn me into a writer with all her enthusiasm and exceptional teaching skills.

And the two wonderfully talented, lovely gentlemen. Alan Midgley who one day said, "I'll design the cover for you". He did, magnificently, and the spine and the back and I drove him insane, and he still loves me.

Andy Lennard for the illustrations. His wonderful sense of humour gives a glimpse to some of the places and people I wrote about.

Rowena Dymond at Resolution Design Ltd for all her kindness.

The marvellous James and Joe at Spiffing Covers for their patience, support and invaluable help.

Kenneth, my Scotsman, my rock, and the most wonderful, loving support.

ANGIE REID

Angie Reid lives in Bristol with her
beloved Scotsman, Kenneth.

She has two children Guy and Nessie,
who keep her grounded, joyful and
constantly inspired.

Travelling around the world has
nourished and fed her desire to meet as
many people as possible.

Printed in Great Britain
by Amazon